State Level Public Enterprises in Sikkim

About the Authors

Dr R.K. Mishra, Senior Professor and Director, Institute of Public Enterprise, Hyderabad, is a graduate of International Management Programme, SDA Bocconi, Milan, Italy. He has been a Fellow of British Council and Commonwealth Secretariat, He has been awarded Fellowships by UNDESA, ICSSR and UGC. He has had research stints at London Business School and Maison Des Sciences De L' Hommes, Paris. He has taught at the University of Bradford, United Kingdom and was a visiting Professor at Maison Des Sciences De L' Hommes, Paris. He is a member of the UN Task Force on International Taskforce on Standards of Excellence in Public Administration and Education. He has been a Management Consultant to several organizations including PWC, DFID, Adam Smith Institute, London, WB, ADB and Centre for Good Governance. He was associated with the UNDP project on Macro Economics of Poverty Reduction carried out by RBI Indira Gandhi Institute of Development Banking and Research. He is Vice-President, International Association of Schools and Institutes in Administration, Brussels. He is on the Steering Committee of Network of Asia-Pacific Schools and Institutes of Public Administration and Governance supported by the Asian Development Bank. He is Honorary Member on the Board of Research, American Biographical Institute, USA. He has handled assignments for the Ministry of Finance, Ministry of Power, Ministry of Trade and Commerce, Ministry of Heavy Industry and Public Enterprises, and Ministry of Finance (Department of Disinvestment). He was a member of the Committee on MIS for Performance Appraisal set up by the Chief Minister of Andhra Pradesh. He was also a member of the working group on privatization set up by the International Institute of Administrative Sciences, Belgium. He has also been a researcher for Planning Commission. Finance Commission, Prime Minister's Economic Advisory Council, OECD, United Nations University—World Institute for Economic Development Research, International Civil Service Consortium, State Bureaus of Public Enterprises, Financial Institutions and Banks. He is Chairman of the Research Committee on Management of the Academy of Social Sciences. His current interests include E-governance, modernization of State, civil service systems, financial administration, human resource administration, environmental administration, privatization and restructuring, poverty management and good governance.

Ms. J. Kiranmai is currently Research Associate at the Institute of Public Enterprise, Hyderabad. She is presently working on the Database on Central Public Enterprises and State Level Public Enterprises in India.

State Level Public Enterprises in Sikkim

(Policy and Planning)

R.K. Mishra
J. Kiranmai

CONCEPT PUBLISHING COMPANY, NEW DELHI-110059

Cataloging in Publication Data—DK
Courtesy: D.K. Agencies (P) Ltd. <docinfo@dkagencies.com>

Mishra, R. K. (Ram Kumar), 1948-
State level public enterprises in Sikkim : policy and planning / R.K. Mishra, J. Kiranmai.
p. cm.
Includes index.
ISBN 8180693961

1. Government business enterprises—India— Sikkim—Planning. 2. Privatization—India—Sikkim. I. Kiranmai, J., joint author. II. Title.

DDC 338.749 541 67 22

ISBN 81-8069-396-1 (HB)

First Published 2007

Published and Printed by
Ashok Kumar Mittal
Concept Publishing Company,
A/15-16, Commercial Block, Mohan Garden,
New Delhi-110059 (INDIA)

Phones : 25351460, 25351794
Fax : 091-11-25357103
Email : publishing@conceptpub.com

Preface

This volume is a modest attempt to study the working of the State Level Public Enterprises (SLPEs) in Sikkim with a point of view to judge their suitability for the retention, closure and privatization in the portfolio of the State. The volume presents a detailed study of each and every enterprise, outlines their strengths and weaknesses and underlines the prospects of these enterprises in terms of their survival. A novel approach has been adopted to complete this study. Besides, an on-the-spot study of all the SLPEs, the Chief Executive Officers (CEOs) of these enterprises were contacted and a rapport was established with the systems controlling such enterprises in the Government. The information collected through questionnaires, interviews, interactions, observations and field visits was juxtaposed on the conceptual framework of restructuring and privatization especially evolved for the study.

The authors are grateful to the Asian Development Bank, National Institute of Public Finance and Policy, CEOs of SLPEs in Sikkim, State Government Officials of the various administrative departments for their kind support and guidance. They are indebt to Prof. M. Govind Rao, Director, National Institute of Public Finance and Policy, Dr A. Premchand, former Director, Expenditure Division, International Monetary Fund and Dr. Pratap Ranjan Jena, Senior Economist, National Institute of Public Finance and Policy for their comments, suggestions and support in completing the study. The authors acknowledge the support received at the Institute of Public Enterprises. However, they alone are responsible for the facts and opinions expressed in the volume.

R.K. Mishra
J. Kiranmai

Contents

Executive Summary

- The State Level Public Enterprise (SLPEs) are an important component of the economy of the State of Sikkim. 22 SLPEs covered in this study had an investment of Rs 726.06 crore as on March 31, 2004. The time is ripe for the policy makers to have a fresh look about the portfolio for retention of the SLPEs.
- A study of the categorization and objectives of the SLPEs shows that the government company form is the most preferred method of organization used to set up the SLPEs.
- The manufacturing enterprise dominated the overall number of the SLPEs, followed by trade and service, utility, welfare and promotional enterprises.
- In terms of market structure, 11 SLPEs were competitive and an equal number of enterprises were non-competitive.
- The SLPEs had 6036 employees on the muster rolls. The casual and muster roll workers exceeded the number of managerial personnel.
- The utility sector SLPEs accounted for 85 per cent of the total investment followed by manufacturing, financial, promotional, welfare, and trade and service enterprises.
- The financial performance of the SLPEs was discouraging in that they were in the red as a whole and also registered accumulated losses and thereby faced capital erosion.
- The resource use was very low registering a declining trend. It was 14.51 per cent, 14.54 per cent and 14.51 per cent in 2001-02, 2002-03 and 2003-04, respectively.
- The SLPEs were characterized by the presence of sub-standard assets, contingent liabilities and weak professional management.
- There is a need to have a fresh look at the SLPEs portfolio through financial, marketing, human resource development, operations and technological restructuring.
- The Government of Sikkim (GoS) policy on restructuring for the SLPEs includes elements such as rationale, objectives, benefits, criteria and procedure for their disinvestment/ privatisation.

- The GoS proposes to privatise/disinvest all non-strategic SLPEs on case to case basis following the criteria laid down to judge as to which enterprise is strategic in nature.
- The SLPEs could be classified for retention and privatisation/disinvestment based on the two dimensional matrix (Market Structure and Financial Success being the two dimensions) and three dimensional matrix (social purpose, resource mobilisation and profitability being the three dimensions).
- The application of the two models provides the same choice for the portfolio for retention of the SLPEs in the State of Sikkim which facilitates our task of outlining the modalities for restructuring and privatisation.
- The application of the restructuring models clearly point out a vast scope for policy and managerial reforms for the SLPEs that are required to be retained in the medium and long-term by the GoS and privatisation/disinvestment of un-strategic SLPEs.
- The application of these models provides eight categories containing 22 enterprises. No enterprise was high on all the parameters. Eight enterprises were low on all the parameters. Fourteen enterprises belonged to the other six categories. The anticipated benefits of the categorization point out that whereas nine enterprises require to be privatised/wound up, the remaining enterprises need to be retained in the public sector. However, the enterprises to be retained need to undergo various kinds of restructuring.
- In view of convenience and ease, the non-strategic enterprises are more amenable for privatisation.
- In order to effect restructuring for privatisation, disinvestment and retention, some legal, accounting and financial requirements need to be fulfilled besides pledging the political commitment.
- A study of the management and operations of the SLPEs reveals that: their social purpose is very low; departmental enterprises dominate the investment scenario; the utility enterprises have a major chunk of investment; their wage cost is very high; no R&D facilities exist in these enterprises; financial and management systems are not in vogue; strengths are far less as compared to weaknesses and so is the case between opportunities and threats; government-enterprise

interface is very low; and most of the enterprises have not formulated performance improvement plans.

- The investments in the SLPEs have become unproductive and cost the GoS Rs 190.52 crore in 2003-04. The returns were negative also in the years 2001-02 and 2002-03. The GoS must unlock the value hidden in the SLPEs by initiating the following measures:
  - A study of the objectives and the profile of the enterprises very clearly reveals the duplication of activities in the case of Sikkim Consumer Co-operative Society, the Denjong Agricultural Co-operative Society, Sikkim State Co-operative Supply and Marketing Federation and State Trading Corporation. *It is suggested that State Trading Corporation Ltd and Sikkim Consumer Co-operative Society be privatised/wound up as they are involved in non-core business activity. The State should not set up any enterprise in future intended to take up a non-core activity.*
  - Although some enterprises serve high social purpose, they duplicate activities or are engaged in non-core activities. The Denjong Agricultural Co-operative Society and Sikkim State Co-operative Supply and Marketing Federation need to be merged to avoid the duplication. The Sikkim Handloom and Handicraft Dev. Corp. Ltd should also concentrate on promotional activities and reduce its direct involvement in sale or manufacturing of handloom and handicrafts items.
  - All the manufacturing enterprises (excepting Sikkim Co-operative Milk Producers Union and Tea Board of Sikkim) have been found low on public purpose, resource mobilisation and profitability. These consist of Sikkim Jewels Ltd, Sikkim Hatchery Ltd, Sikkim Poultry Dev. Corp. Ltd, Sikkim Precision Industries, Govt. Fruit Preservation Company and Sikkim Time Corporation. Sikkim Power Dev. Corp., also forms a part of this category. These enterprises may be privatised/wound up.
  - The utility sector enterprises viz., Sikkim Nationalized Transport and Sikkim Energy and Department of Power form the lifeline of the State and need therefore to be retained in the public sector. However, their corporatisation is necessary. Once they are corporatised,

OPTIMA (Optimal Performance through Internal Management Action) could be introduced in these enterprises.

- The welfare and promotional enterprises have to be continued in the state sector as they deal with the up-liftment of the down trodden classes of society and development of certain economic activity. It is in this backdrop that SABCCO, Khadi and Villages Industries Board and Sikkim Tourism Dev. Corp. could be retained in the portfolio of public sector by the GoS.
- The financial enterprises such as SIDICO, State Bank of Sikkim and Sikkim State Co-operative Bank provide financial input for the economic development and hence could be retained. However, they should formulate performance improvement plans for greater effectiveness.
- The suggested status of the SLPEs has been given at Table 6.2.
- The government control and direction relating to the SLPEs in Sikkim is lacking. Although an official of the level of the Director in the Finance Department has been made responsible for coordinating the enterprise-government interface, he is saddled with several responsibilities and finds no time to attend to the issues relating to the SLPEs. The finance department may borrow the services of a surplus official to appoint him as the Director (SLPEs) who may be charged with the responsibility of inter-departmental coordination, preparation of an annual survey on the SLPEs, formulation of management development and training plans, and provide support for clearing the arrears of accounts, etc.
- The Director (SLPEs) should look into the problems of manpower planning, wage policies, internal audit and control systems in the SLPEs. He may work for the introduction of the Memorandum of Understanding (MoU) to remedy the problems of accountability and performance evaluation. He should also organize training in project evaluation and project management.
- To improve the quality of corporate governance the laws governing the SLPEs viz., Registration of Companies Act of Sikkim and the Income Tax Act of Sikkim should be integrated with the laws of the main land.

- The board composition should be balanced with the representation of professional directors, user interests, employee representatives, and the government nominees. The board size should be limited between seven and twelve comprising government not exceeding a number of more than two at the maximum. The position of managing director and chairman needs to be combined. The separation of the post of chairman-cum-managing director has resulted in wasteful expenditure and unhealthy organisational culture.
- For the enterprises to be retained, OPTIMA needs to be introduced to synergies the management action through costing, budgeting, pricing, auditing, MIS, manpower planning and recruitment, training and management development, labour adjustments and performance evaluation.
- To decide about the modalities of privatisation/winding up of non-core enterprises, a restructuring board on the pattern of Karnataka, Maharashtra, Punjab, and Andhra Pradesh, may be set up to deal with each enterprises, in this regard, on case by case basis.
- The GoS may formulate a scheme of social safety net for the SLPEs to provide support to work force affected by labour adjustments. The Director (SLPEs) may be entrusted with the responsibility of formulating and implementing the social safety net programme (SSNP). A special fund of Rs 10 crore may be created for this and other related purposes and placed with Director (SLPEs).

• The total funds requirement for the restructuring of the SLPEs would be Rs 222.03 crore (composed of Rs 236.98 crore of gross restructuring cost –Rs 24.96 crore of restructuring cost of enterprise to be privatised/wound up +Rs 10 crore as the macro restructuring fund to be kept at the disposal of the Director (SLPEs). The GoS may provide a one-time restructuring grant to the enterprises for restructuring. This grant could be disbursed over a period of three years in a ratio of 34:33:33 amounting to Rs 75.48 crore, Rs 73.27 crore and Rs 73.27 crore depending on the urgency, absorption capacity of the enterprise and the availability of the resources with the government.

Policy Matrix

Issue	*Proposed action*
Investments in SLPEs	• Sound investment appraisal • Effective project management
Existence of departmental enterprises	• Corporatisation
Presence of non-competitive SLPEs	• Introducing competitive measures such as strategic business units (SBUs), joint ventures, etc. • Reorganising large enterprises • Private sector development • Attracting successful private sector groups
Presence of excessive labour force	• Labour adjustments • Safety net • De-linking SLPEs salaries scales from the GoS scales • Appropriate recruitment policy discouraging appointment of deputationists and also safeguarding SLPEs against becoming dumping ground of personnel lacking competencies
Discouraging financial performance	• Return on investment oriented functioning • Improved working capital productivity • Reduction in interest and wage costs

Issue	*Proposed action*
:ationalisaiton of ariff structure	• Cost oriented prices • Cost audit • Social purpose cost reimbursement • Restraint on cross subsidization
ow resource use	• Increase in market share • Product/service development • Customer relationship management • Reduction in fixed and working capital
'oor accounting ystems	• Timely finalization of accounts • Greater disclosure • Professional accounting staff
:etention of SLPEs ı public portfolio	• Low social purpose, low resource mobiliser, low or no profit earning SLPEs could be privatised/wound up • High social purpose, high resource mobiliser, high profit earning SLPEs could be retained • SLPEs in other categories could be restructured • Promotional, financial and welfare enterprises should continue to be retained • Embargo on new non-core enterprise
Jn-productivity of ıvestments	• Enterprises duplicating activities could be merged • Non-core enterprises could be privatised/wound up • Initiation of Performance improvement plans
Veak Government ontrol and direction	• Services of an officer be used as the Director (SLPEs) who may be assigned the responsibility of: o inter-departmental co-ordination, o preparation of annual survey on the SLPEs,

Issue	*Proposed action*
	○ formulation and implementation of management and development plans, ○ provided support for clearing arrears of accounts, ○ Manpower planning, ○ Wage policies, ○ Internal audit and control systems, ○ Introduction and implementation of MoU • Training in project evaluation and management
Unsatisfactory quality of corporate governance	• Integration of the Registration of Companies Act of Sikkim and Income Tax Act of Sikkim with the central acts. • Balanced composition of boards • Combining the post of Chairman and Managing Director to Chairman-cum-Managing Director
Systemic weakness	• Introducing Optimum Performance Through Internal Management Action (OPTIMA) • Introducing/strengthening internal audit, budgeting, pricing, performance evaluation and MoU systems • Replacing paternalistic style by modern management models.
Modalities of privatisation of non-core enterprises	• Setting up a restructuring board on the pattern of Karnataka, Punjab, Maharashtra and Andhra Pradesh to approve modalities on case-by-case basis
Social Safety Net Programme (SSNP)	• Director (SLPEs) be entrusted with the responsibility of SSNP • A special fund of Rs 10 crore be created for SSNP and other related purposes

1

Sikkim: Socio-Economic Profile

1.1 History of Sikkim

Sikkim was inhabited in pre-historic times by three tribes namely Naong, Chang and the Mon. Later, Lepcha entered the state and the tribes completely. The origin of Lepchas reveals that they belonged to the clan of the Nagas of the Mikir, Garo and Khasia hills which lie to the south of the Brahamaputra valley i.e., somewhere on the borders of Tibet and Burma. Later many kings from Bhutan, China, Tibet invaded the State till 19th century. During 19th century, the defeat of Nepalese by the Chinese did little to weaken the expansionist designs of the Nepal. The Nepalese continued to make attacks into the neighbouring British territories in India. British India successfully befriended Sikkim. They felt that by doing so the 74 expanding powers of the Gorkhas would be curtailed. Britishers were keen in establishing trade link with Tibet and the route through Sikkim was the most feasible one. The war between Nepal and British India broke out in 1814 and came to an end in 1816 with the defeat of the Nepalese and the subsequent signing of the Treaty of Sugauli. British India signed another treaty with Sikkim in 1817 known as the Treaty of Titalia in which former territories, which the Nepalese captured, were restored to Sikkim. During 1884, Britishers explored the possibility of trade routes to Tibet through the Lachen Valley. The Britishers started building of roads in Sikkim. This was viewed with suspicion by Tibet and in 1886, some Tibetan militia occupied Lingtu in Sikkim near Jelepla pass. In May 1888, the Tibetans attacked Gnathang below Jelepla but were driven away. In September of the same year the British called for reinforcements and the Tibetans were pushed back from Lingtu. The Britishers appointed Claude White as the first political officer to Sikkim during 1889 and Chogyal Thutob Namgyal was virtually under his supervision. The growing Russian influence in Tibet, the British sent an expedition in 1904. The expedition met with resistance from the Tibetan army, which was defeated, and a treaty was dictated by Younghusband on Tibet. The Treaty secured monopoly-trading privileges in Tibet for the British India.

After 1947, India became independent. Tashi Namgyal was successful in getting a special status of protectorate for Sikkim. This was in face of stiff resistance from local parties like Sikkim State Congress who wanted a democratic setup and accession of Sikkim to the Union of India. The treaty signed between India and Sikkim ratified the status of Sikkim as a protectorate with Chogyal as the Monarch. Tashi Namgyal died in 1963 and was succeeded by his son Palden Thondup Namgyal. There were rumbling in the political ranks and file of the State in 1970, which demanded the removal of Monarchy and the establishment of a democratic setup. Finally culminated in wide spread agitation against Sikkim Durbar in 1973. There was a complete collapse in the administration. The Indian Government tried to bring about a semblance of order in the State by appointing a Chief Administrator Mr. B. S. Das. Further, events and election led to Sikkim becoming transformed from a protectorate to an associate State. On 4th September 1947, the leader of Sikkim Congress, Kazi Lendup Dorji, was elected as the Chief Minister of the State. However, the Chogyal remained as the constitutional figure head monarch in the new setup. Events leading to the confrontation between the Chogyal and the popular Government caused Sikkim to become a full-fledged 22nd state of the Indian Union on 16th May 1975. The Institution of Chogyal was subsequently abolished.

Since then Sikkim has been a State of the Indian Union. In the 1979 assembly elections, Mr. Nar Bahadur Bhandari, was elected as the Chief Minister of Sikkim.

1.2 Sikkim: An Overview

The total area of Sikkim is 7,096 sq. km. Sikkim covers barely 0.22 per cent of the total geographical area of India, but offers avenues for the intrepid investor, which few others can match. Lying between 27 to 28 degree North latitude and 88 to 89 degree East on longitude, this Himalayan State is bordered by West Bengal on the South, China on the North, Nepal on the West and Bhutan on the East. The land is criss-crossed by energetic mountain streams, extravagant valleys and decorated by a profusion of exotic orchids and the brilliant rhododendrons.

The 2001 Census of India records Sikkim's population at 5,40,493. Literacy stands at an impressive 65.1 per cent with the State Government continually focusing on improving it further. In 1991, Sikkim ranked first in its rural literacy rate, which stood at 61.4 per cent then and has improved since.

1.3 Natural Resources and Economic Profile

The main crops produced in Sikkim are Rice, Wheat, Maize, Cardamom and Ginger. There are also a plethora of exotic flowers and orchids that grow wild in Sikkim forests and can be easily incorporated into greenhouses by intelligent entrepreneurs. The environment is unpolluted and the State is committed to heralding industrialization without tampering its ecological balance. Abundant hydro-power potential of 8,000 MW, promising tourism potential, high literacy rate, vast natural resources like an impressive forest cover and lavish mineral deposits are clear indicators that Sikkim is making steady headway towards all round development. Animal husbandry and Agriculture continue to be the mainstay to the people's livelihood with even the existing industries capitalizing on Sikkim's agro-based and handicrafts potential. The banking sector is well developed in the State with almost all nationalized banks having a branch in Sikkim and new ones opening up offices here in impressive frequency. A full-fledged industries and commerce department is also in place to help any interested investor and an industrial policy has also been framed and implemented in the State. The State has good resource base of minerals like zinc, lead, copper, dolomite, coal quartzite, graphite, talc etc. Commercial exploitation of some of these minerals was carried out by the state agencies.

1.4 Economic Growth and Development

Economic development in Sikkim, as indicated by the growth rate of the State Domestic Product (SDP), has been very impressive, averaging almost 10 per cent per annum, over the past two decades. In spite of a relatively high growth of population of 2.85 per cent per annum during 1981-91 and 3.30 per cent per annum during 1991-2001, per capita income has increased by almost a hundred and fifty per cent during this period. High growth rate has been sustained during the 1990s. According to the Tenth Plan of the State, Gross State Domestic Product (GSDP) growth has been over seven per cent and per capita income growth three and a half per cent per annum over the period 1993-94 to 1999-00 (PDD, 2001). Sikkim's performance in the spheres of education and health has also been impressive. As a result, Human Development Index (HDI).

Table 1.1 shows the sectoral plan allocation in Sikkim since 1954-2002. In the first Seven Year Plan (1954-61) and the two Five Year Plans (1961-66 and 1966-71), which were financed by the Government of India, planned development was outside the revenue-expenditure processes of the State Budget. In the Ninth Five Year Plan, as compared to Rs 32.4 million in the First Plan, it increased to Rs 16 billion (about 500 fold). This is also almost 122 per cent increase over the Eight Plan outlay of Rs 7.2 billion.

Agriculture and allied activities have been the mainstay of the majority of the people receiving on an average 20 per cent of the total plan outlay up to the Seventh Plan. Since then this crucial sector's share has shown a tendency to decline, being as low as 13.6 per cent in Eight Plan. Power Sector has a share of almost 20 per cent—double of what it was during the entire plan period since 1954. The other vital infrastructural area of roads and bridges has fallen to less than 10 per cent. Further, though some social sectors, e.g. education, have improved their share, allocation to health has been low. The expenditure on social services amounted to 2.0384 billion in 1999-00, which represented 13.19 per cent of the total revenue expenditure.

1.5 Net State Domestic Product

The economic growth at a macro level is reflected both in its GDP and per-capita income. Table 1.2 shows that both GDP and per capita income at constant prices recorded a steady increase during the period from 1980-1992, the highest growth in 1987

Table 1.1: Sectoral and sub-sectoral plan allocation in Sikkim (1954-2002)

Sectors	*I Plan (1954-61)%*	*II Plan (1961-66)%*	*III Plan (1966-71)%*	*IV Plan (1971-75)%*	*V Plan (1974-79)%*	*VI Plan (1980-85)%*	*VII Plan (1992-97)*	*VIII Plan (1992-97)%*	*IX Plan (1998-02)%*
Agriculture & Allied Activities	21.5	20.0	15.0	14.2	15.9	26.0	21.1	13.6	17.1
Power	9.2	8.3	7.3	8.8	10.0	9.4	17.4	24.9	19.4
Industries	4.3	0.5	6.7	3.5	6.6	4.2	4.0	3.85	4.2
Roads & Bridges	42.8	40.5	43.4	36.3	26.1	22.3	6.4	14.8	9.6
Road Transport	5.2	6.9	4.1	3.5	3.1	4.9	3.2	1.85	0.8
Education	7.4	12.4	7.9	8.8	7.4	7.0	12.2	10.7	12.5
Health	7.1	7.2	9.4	4.1	4.5	3.5	2.5	1.11	3.1
Tourism	–	0.8	0.4	4.4	2.0	1.5	0.9	15.2	3.59
Others*	2.5	3.4	5.8	16	24.4	21.2	32.3	14.0	29.7
Total Outlay (Rs Millions)	32.4	63.7	97.1	203.6	401.0	1478.0	2824.0	7245.0	16028.0

Note: *Others include rural development, irrigation and flood control, communications and other social, general and economic services

Source: Computed from various Plan Documents, Government of Sikkim, Gangtok.

Table 1.2: Sikkim: Net State Domestic Product and Per Capita Income at constant prices

Years	*Domestic Product (Rs thousand)*	*Annual Growth Rate %*	*Per capita income (Rs thousand)*	*Annual Growth Rate %*
1980-81	489,800	—	157,100	—
1981-82	521,900	6.55	161,100	2.55
1982-83	588,200	12.70	175,000	8.63
1983-84	614,200	4.42	175,800	0.46
1984-85	694,600	13.09	191,900	9.16
1985-86	755,900	8.82	201,700	5.11
1986-87	891,700	17.96	229,700	13.88
1987-88	1075,500	20.61	267,800	16.59
1988-89	1149,000	6.83	292,400	9.19
1989-90	1228,900	5.51	311,800	6.63
1990-91	1353,200	10.11	336,900	8.05
1991-92	1442,900	6.63	349,200	3.65

Source: Ministry of Finance, Economic Survey, Government of India, various issues.

1.6 Industrial Policy and Infrastructure

The Industrial sector was not well developed in Sikkim during the pre-merger period. Distillation of wines and liquors was one of the first modern industries established at Singtam in 1955, providing employment to 30 managers and 150 labourers by the Third Plan period. This distillery was equipped with the state-of-the art equipment and served both domestic and overseas markets. The other undertaking that for yours was a flagship company' was the Government Fruit Preservation Factory also set up at Singtam in 1956. This factory utilized the ample orange production in the State, cutting down wastage in transit and storage locally, and eliminating middlemen.

There are no Central Public Sector Undertakings in Sikkim. However, the Industry Department shows that there are 1360 units which have been granted provisional registration from 1976 onwards. Out of these, less than 300 Small Scale Industries and tiny units have begun to function. Over 72 per cent of these units are located in the East district. Table 1.3 shows region wise Registered Small Scale Units since 1975.

Table 1.3: Registered Small Scale Industries/Units

Period	*East*	*North*	*South*	*West*	*SSI/Tiny Units*
1975/76-79/80	7	2	–	1	10
1980/81-84/85	7	4	2	13	–
1985/86-89/90	56	4	14	9	80
1990/91-94/95	84	1	18	11	115
1995/96-98/99	60	–	13	6	79

Source: Government of Sikkim, Department of Industry, Gangtok.

1.7 Sikkim's Industrial Policy 1996

In view of the Government for speedy industrial development and generation of adequate employment opportunities through self-employment, a comprehensive industries policy for Sikkim has been formulated as follows:

Policy Objectives

The policy envisages:

- Creation of an atmosphere conducive to industrial growth, taking into consideration the availability natural resources and the local socio-economic environment.
- Maintenance of the Green State image while promoting industrial activities.
- Rehabilitation of sick industries with comprehensive assistance and guidance from the Department of Industry and privatisation of selecting State Public Sector Undertaking.
- Enrichment of the agricultural sector through the establishment of appropriate linkage between agriculture and agro-based industries.
- Ensuring balanced regional development through promotion of Khadi, Village, Cottage and Tiny, Small and Ancillary industries.
- Promotion of the traditional handloom handicrafts and artisan sector, by providing adequate support in the form of common facilities like service centers cheap raw material, technical inputs, marketing network skill development, etc.

- Development of tourism as an industry.
- Development of Sikkim as a major centre for manufacture and marketing of tea.
- Rapid Development of basic infrastructure so that industrial growth is facilitated.
- Encouraging self-employment and identification of avenues for the same by providing guidance through data bank of project-profiles and other related information.
- Promote and encourage high-value, low-volume products, in view of the transportation-bottlenecks in the States.
- Human resource development through appropriate skill and entrepreneurship development programmes behavioural training etc. at district sub-division and block level, to meet the emergent skill requirements of the State within a stipulated time frame.
- Protection and promotion of interest of the local people especially at the unskilled and semi-skilled levels by defining norms for a minimum percentage of employment to the local people in the industrial units.
- Encouraging joint ventures between local entrepreneurs and industrialist from outside the State for setting up industries within industrial belt area.
- Simplification of procedures and opening up of Sikkim with a view to attract both internal and outside the State for setting up of industries within industrial belt area.

Strategy for Implementation of the Policy

The objects set out in the industrial policy challenging and require a well-defined strategy implementation. The government proposes to achieve these objectives by pursuing the following strategies:

- Identification of thrust areas and effective promotion of industries in these areas.
- Announcement of attractive package and fiscal incentives.
- Special promotional measures for rural and traditional industry.
- Establishing industrial estates and growth centers to facilitate integrated development of industry.
- Development of rehabilitation package for the industries.

- Revamping the public sector undertakings.
- Creation of appropriate organization arrangements.
- Development of marketing support systems.
- Development of appropriate training facilities.
- Creation of single window agency.

Identification of Thrust Areas

The State has identified certain thrust industries for concentrated industrial development, which will enjoy additional incentives, and are as follows:

- Agro-based industries
- Floriculture
- Animal Husbandry and Diary Products
- Minor Forest Based Produce
- Handloom, Handicrafts and Village Industries
- Tourism
- Precision oriented, high value, low volume products
- Electronic and software
- Hydel Power
- Tea

Attractive Packages and Fiscal Incentives

To generate an entrepreneurial spirit and encourage investments in industry, the Government announces an attractive package of incentives and facilities, keeping in mind the increase in competition among the various States.

Special Promotional Measures for Rural and Traditional Industry

The rural non-farm sector has been identified as critical area for achieving national goals and for the creation of employment. This also provides for generation and distribution of income to the backward rural districts of any state. Rural industries comprise enterprises owned by rural entrepreneurs in agricultural and semi-urban regions and are sub-sectors of small scale enterprises and constitute micro enterprises. Some potential areas include flower procession, hereby processing, sericulture, spices and oilseeds processing, cane and bamboo products, power etc. Special promotional measures will be undertaken by the State Government to strengthen these sectors.

Traditional industries like Cottage, Handlooms and Handicrafts and Khadi Industries will be further encouraged. A comprehensive review of the existing institutional arrangement has been undertaken and suitable measures adopted for achieving the policy objectives. The Sikkim Khadi and Village Industries Board is proposed to be revamped.

Industrial Estate and Growth Centre to Facilitate Integrated Development of Industry

The government has encouraged the setting up of self-contained industrial estates and growth centers to facilitate an integrated approach towards optimization of available resources and infrastructure, including creation of infrastructure, marketing facilities and communication networks. The responsibilities related to infrastructure development is undertaken by the Directorate of Industries and the efforts are being made for the development of supportive infrastructure like roads, power, water supply etc. for such estates. Adequate budget provision has been allotted for this purpose by the viable units.

Development of a Rehabilitation Package for the Sick Industries

There are large numbers of sick industries in the state and the government intends to introduce enterprise specific schemes for their rehabilitation. The viability of each unit is proposed to be individually studied to determine whether it should be operated by the original promoters, new management, as joint ventures with the government. A model rehabilitation package has been developed for the rejuvenation of the viable units.

Revamping the Public Sector Undertakings

The government proposes to undertake the review of ventures only in the core sectors and in keeping with the policies of the Central Government, some of the public sector undertaking are proposed to be privatized. The state enterprises in the core/thrust sectors are proposed to be revamped to improve their efficiency and functioning.

Sikkim Industrial Development and Investment Corporation is to play a more active role in the industrialization process in the state. It is engaged in providing escort services to entrepreneur proposing to set up projects valued at Rs. 50 lakhs and above.

Organizational Arrangements

The strategy for industrial development is proposed to be achieved when it is implemented through appropriate organizational facilities. Industrial promotion in Sikkim will be handled by the Director of Industries. The promotion of individual secotrs like handlooms, handicrafts, agriculture etc. will be the responsibility of the respective departments in coordination with the Director of industries.

Re-organization of the Directorate of Industries

The Directorate of Industries plays a key role in facilitating and co-ordinating activities related industrial development. The services to be provided by District Industries Centres are intended to include area planning for rural industrialization, activity on finance, organization production, technology and marketing assistance for submission of loan applications, speedy clearance for new industries, project supervision and management training programmes etc. The District Industries Centre, also promotes and encourages creation of representation organization to offer services on market information, marketing quality testing, production development, processing etc. Design and Service Centres have been created under the District Industries Centre to provide designs and know-how for the development of suitable products by engaging technically qualified personnel at the block level. Community poly-techniques are being involved in efforts of skill up-gradation, development of work culture, technology orientation creation of pilot project, with the help of voluntary organizations.

The Rehabilitation Cell of the Department of Industries, along with Sikkim Industrial Development and Investment Corporation, actively participates in analyzing the viability of the sick units in the State and suggest measures for their rehabilitation.

A Public Enterprises Cell has been constituted in the Directorate of Industries to oversees the efficient functioning of the public sector units and formulate guidelines for their employees and fund management and organizational and structural adjustments.

The Industries Training Institute have been brought under the purview of the Directorate of Industries to improve its functioning and impart training as per the requirement of the industries in the state.

Sikkim Investment Promotion Committee

A high powered Sikkim Investment Promotion Committee (SIPC) has been constituted with the Chief Secretary of the State as its Chairman and the concerned Department Secretaries as other Board members, along with the Development Commissioner, Finance Secretary, Secretary Industries and Director Industries.

On receiving a proposal whose total project cost is greater than Rs 75 lakhs from any department or public sector unit, the Directorate of Industries undertakes a critical assessment of the proposal and forward it to SIPC with its recommendations. Proposal cleared by SIPC are only be placed in the Council of Ministers for a decision.

Development of Marketing

There are a number of marketing organizations in the State such as the State Trading Corporation of Sikkim, Sikkim State Co-operative Supply and Marketing Federation Ltd. In addition, a Marketing and Export Promotion Council (MEPC) is proposed to be set up to support the sale of goods within and outside the State. It will be the apex agency for the issues of detailed guidelines for marketing activities in the State.

Policy Interventions and Suggestions

The Government of Sikkim constituted a Task Force under the Chairmanship of Commissioner-cum-Secretary, Department of Industries on 15-5-1999. The Task Force recommendations of indicate the changing face of policy interventions in the industrial sector of the State. The following some of the important recommendations are:

- The State Government must coax the primary sector into generating surpluses so that the purchasing power can come into the hands of the rural masses and in turn fan industrial growth.
- It is estimated that Sikkim needs to generate about 6,500 jobs per annum.

1.8 New Industrial Policy, 2003

In the New Industrial Policy 2003, the Government of Sikkim has requested for a special package for development of industries in the state on the lines for the North East Industrial Policy. The Government had discussions on Strategy and Action Plan for Development of Industries and generation of employment in the State of Sikkim were held with the various related Ministries on the issues *inter alia*, infrastructure development, financial concessions and easy market access.

The State of Sikkim lags behind in industrial development, a need has been felt for structured interventionist strategies to accelerate industrial development of the State and boost investor confidence. The new initiatives would provide the require incentives as well as an enabling environment for industrial development, improve availability of capital and increase market access to provide a fillip to the private investment in the State. New industrial units and existing industrial units on the substantial expansion as defined, set up in Growth Center, Industrial Infrastructure Development Centers and other locations like Industrial Estates, Export Processing Zones, Food Parks, IT Parks, etc. as notified by the Central Government are entitled to 100 per cent income tax and excise duty exemption for a period of 10 years format the date of commencement of commercial production.

1.9 Conclusions

Sikkim is an important state in the north-east. It is endowed with a very high potential of industrial development. It has is an emerging state tremendous natural resources in the form of water, people, vegetation and land. With the opening of Nathula pass, the trade links between India and China will receive a great boost and is expected to result in lifting the tempo of industrial development of Sikkim to new levels.

2

State Level Public Enterprises in Sikkim

2.1 Introduction

The State Level Public Enterprise (SLPEs) are an important component of the economy of the State of Sikkim. The finances of the State of Sikkim need strengthening in terms of their allocation and productive deployment. The re-engineering of the state finances has to be done with a human face. The social and economic consequences of the re-engineering have to be kept in the backdrop while designing the strategies for this purpose and implementation of such strategies. The investments in the SLPEs in the State of Sikkim have been increasing over the years. The performance, however, has not kept pace with the expectations. This divergence has adversely affected the state finances. The time is ripe for the policy makers to have a fresh look about the portfolio for retention of the SLPEs.

The study deals with restructuring, divestment and privatisation of the SLPEs in the State of Sikkim through the preparation of the feasibility studies for each enterprise by giving due regard to the socio-economic consequences of such actions. Although, 11 SLPEs were identified for the task, the Government of Sikkim (GoS) added another 11 SLPEs to the list. The GoS further included the Sikkim Nationalized Transport and the Sikkim State Energy and Power Department to the list as they are major commercial activity enablers holding a predominant position in terms of investment, turnover, financial losses incurred and manpower. The Government later decided to exclude the power sector from the scope of the study. However, data on the broder dimensions of the power sector as related to the Sikkim Energy and Power Department and the Sikkim Power Development

Corporation have been included to provide a macro view of the SLPEs. Sikkim Handloom and Handicrafts Development Corporation, Sikkim Hatchery Ltd and Sikkim Poultry Development Corporation Ltd participated in the final lap of the study. The information was collected through the questionnaires on Financial and other related aspects concerning SLPEs (see Annexure 1.9), Schedule on Internal Organisaiton and Structure of SLPEs (see Annexure 1.10), and continuous interaction with the policy makers in the GoS and the top management of the SLPEs.

2.2 Typology

A study of the categorization and objectives of the SLPEs shows that the government company, public corporation, co-operative society and the departmental forms have been used in setting up these enterprises. Most of the enterprises have been established after the integration of Sikkim in the Union of India. The enterprises that existed with the state before integration were Sikkim Nationalized Transport, State Energy and Power Department, State Bank of Sikkim, State Trading Corporation, Sikkim Fruit Preservation Factory, Tea Board of Sikkim Ltd. and the Denjong Agricultural Co-Operative Society Ltd. The all-India pattern enterprises were established soon after the integration of Sikkim. These included Sikkim Jewels, Sikkim Times Company (SITCO), Sikkim Industrial and Investment Development Corporation Ltd. (SIDICO), Sikkim Consumer Co-operative Society, Sikkim State Co-operative Supply and Marketing Federation Ltd. (SIMFED) and Sikkim Co-operative Milk Producers Union Ltd. (Sikkim Milk Union). The 1990s have seen a spurt of activity with regard to the setting up of the SLPEs. In this decade the enterprises set up included Sikkim Tourism Development Corporation Ltd., Sikkim Handloom and Handicrafts Development Corporation, Sikkim Poultry Development Corporation Ltd., Sikkim Hatchery Ltd., Sikkim Precision Industries Ltd, Sikkim Scheduled Castes, Tribes and Other Backward Classes Development Corporation Ltd. (SABCCO), Sikkim Power Development Corporation Ltd. and Sikkim State Consumer Co-operative Bank. The following Table 2.1 provides the details with regard to forms of organization of the SLPEs.

Table 2.1: Typology of SLPEs

Typology	*No. of Enterprises*
Government Company	11
Public Corporation/Boards	4
Co-operative Society	5
Departmental Enterprise	2

Source: Annexure 1.1.

The Government Company form was the most preferred method of setting up the SLPEs. It is, however, important to note that the State of Sikkim continues to have its own Companies Act which was earlier promulgated by the Chogyal in 1961 titled as the Registration of Companies Act.

2.3 Classification

A peep into the objectives of the SLPEs points out that the major purposes of their creation related to undertaking in the state sector manufacturing, trade and services, financial, promotional, welfare and utility sector activities. The manufacturing enterprises dominated the overall number, followed by trade and service, utility, welfare and promotional enterprises. Table 2.2 provides the details with regard to the classification of the SLPEs.

Table 2.2: Classification of SLPEs

Classification	*No. of Enterprises*
Manufacturing	8
Trade and Service	4
Financial	3
Promotional	3
Utility	3
Welfare	1

Source: Annexure 1.1.

2.4 Market Structure

The SLPEs operated in markets varying from competitive to monopoly conditions. Some enterprises enjoyed captive market conditions initially but due to the liberalization policies adopted by the Government of India they are compelled to operate in competitive markets currently. Even in the field of utilities monopoly markets are assuming competitive character due to unbundling/strategic business group approach being adopted in power sector and cold privatisation being followed in the public transport corporations. However, this may not be true of the promotional, welfare and co-operative SLPEs as they have a specific mandate of helping the weaker sections of the society and foster the growth of given activities, on the one hand, and protect the interest of the co-operators, on the other. In terms of market structure, the position of the SLPEs is shown in Figure.

Competitive	*Non-Competitive*
• Sikkim Precision Industries Ltd • State Trading Corporation • Government Fruit Preservation Factory • Sikkim Consumers' Co-operative Society • Sikkim State Co-operative Supply and Marketing Federation Ltd • Sikkim Jewels Ltd • Sikkim Hatchery Ltd • Sikkim Poultry Dev. Corp. Ltd • Sikkim Times Corp. Ltd • Sikkim Co-operative Milk Producers Union Ltd • Sikkim Power Dev. Corp.	• Sikkim Industrial and Investment Development Corp. Ltd • Sikkim State Co-operative Bank • State Bank of Sikkim • Tea Board of Sikkim • Sikkim Tourism Development Corp. Ltd • Sikkim Nationalized Transport • Sikkim State Energy and Power Department • Sikkim Scheduled Castes, Tribes and Other Backward Classes Development Corp. Ltd • Khadi and Village Industries Board • Denjong Agricultural Co-Operative Society Ltd • Sikkim Handloom and Handicrafts Dev. Corp. Ltd

Fig. 2.1: Market Structure
Source: Annexure 1.7.

2.5 Manpower

The departmental enterprises viz., Sikkim Energy and Power Department and Sikkim Nationalized Transport topped the list of SLPEs in terms of providing highest employment among the SLPEs being studied. The casual and muster roll workers far exceeded the number of managerial personnel. The position of the various SLPEs with regard to manpower strength is given in Table 2.3.

Table 2.3: Manpower

Name of the enterprise	*Managerial*	*Non-Managerial*	*Casual*	*Others*	*Total*
Sikkim Industrial and Investment Development Corporation Ltd	19	16	–	–	34
State Bank of Sikkim	50	221	–	–	271
Sikkim State Co-operative Bank	12	4	–	–	16
Sikkim Jewels	20	105	–	–	125
Sikkim Hatchery	1	2	13	–	15
Sikkim Poultry	1	0	5	–	6
Sikkim Precision Industries	4	50	6	–	60
Sikkim Time Company	22	87	37	–	146
Tea Board of Sikkim	5	444	–	–	449
Govt. Fruit Preservation Factory	4	56	3	–	63
Sikkim Co-operative Milk Producers Union Ltd	7	60	16	–	83
Sikkim Tourism	4	85	–	–	89
Sikkim Handloom and Handicrafts Development Corp. Ltd	01	12	–	–	13
Khadi and Village Industries Board	14	69	–	–	83*
State Trading Corp.	11	70	27	–	108
Sikkim Consumer Co-operative Society	2	22	3	–	27
Sikkim State Co-operative Supply and Marketing Federation Ltd	9	23	–	8	40
Denjong Agricultural Co-Operative Society Ltd	2	60	40	–	112
Sikkim Nationalized Transport Corp.	57	767	91	42	824
State Energy and Department of Power	205	3228	–	–	3443
Sikkim Power Dev. Corp.	7	14	–	–	21
SABCCO	4	12	–	–	16
Total	461	5407	241	50	6036

Source: Annexure 1.10.

* This excludes 100 part-time workers.

The SLPEs did not staff themselves with sufficient managerial manpower. The non-managerial staff was in excess of requirements. The work-charged and muster roll employees exposed the SLPEs to weak manpower planning and management. The value added per employee was insignificant and so was the average turnover per employee.

2.6 Investments

Table 2.4 depicts the investments in the SLPEs.

Table 2.4: Investment in SLPEs

(Rs. In crore)

Name of the enterprise	*Classification*	*2001-02*	*2002-03*	*2003-04*
SIDICO	Financial	19.46	19.48	19.66
State Bank of Sikkim	Financial	4.56	4.98	5.40
Sikkim State Co-operative Bank	Financial	8.50	8.91	9.36
	Total	**32.52**	**33.37**	**34.42**
Sikkim Jewels	Manufacturing	7.10	7.82	7.04
Sikkim Hatchery	Manufacturing	0.46	0.46	0.46
Sikkim Poultry	Manufacturing	0.79	0.79	0.79
Sikkim Precision Industries	Manufacturing	0.00	3.70	3.70
SITCO	Manufacturing	11.96	12.03	11.74
Tea Board of Sikkim	Manufacturing	19.52	20.44	22.71
Sikkim Milk Union	Manufacturing	0.10	0.14	0.14
Govt. Fruit Preservation Factory	Manufacturing	0.76	1.07	0.00
	Total	**40.69**	**45.20**	**41.63**
Sikkim Tourism	Promotional	4.79	4.79	6.06
Sikkim Handloom and Handicrafts Dev. Corp	Promotional	0.00	0.00	0.80
Khadi and Village Industries Board	Promotional	10.09	11.24	12.01
	Total	**14.88**	**16.03**	**18.87**
State Trading Corp.	Trade and Service	1.11	1.11	1.11
Sikkim Consumer Co-operative Society	Trade and Service	0.17	0.17	0.17
SIMFED	Trade and Service	1.05	1.01	1.02
Denjong Agricultural Co-Operative Society Ltd	Trade and Service	0.20	0.20	0.20
	Total	**2.53**	**2.49**	**2.50**

(Contd)

Table 2.4 (*Contd*)

Name of the enterprise	*Classification*	*2001-02*	*2002-03*	*2003-04*
Sikkim Nationalized Transport Corp.	Utility	33.08	34.49	34.39
State Energy and Department of Power	Utility	470.92	470.92	514.79
Sikkim Power Dev. Corp.	Utility	53.01	53.01	53.01
	Total	557.01	558.42	602.19
SABCCO	Welfare	15.61	20.10	21.50
	Total	15.61	20.10	21.50
	Grand Total	**663.24**	**676.86**	**726.06**

Source: Annexure 1.1, 1.2 and 1.3.

The analysis of investments in the SLPEs points to the following:

- The total investments in the SLPEs increased form Rs 663.24 crore in 2001-02 to Rs 726.06 crore in 2003-04
- About 85 per cent of the total investments was made in the utility sector enterprises
- The manufacturing enterprises followed by the financial enterprises come next in the pecking order.
- In terms of investments in the various forms of the SLPEs, the departmental enterprises shared about 81 per cent and the government companies had 11 per cent of the total investment. The other forms of the SLPEs had only nine per cent of the total investment.
- The promotional, welfare, and trade and service enterprises carry small investments.
- The enterprises in all the sectors have conveniently ignored the principle of leverage leading to an inadequate debt-equity mix.

Table 2.5 shows that a large number of enterprises did not have any debt and therefore ended up with nil debt-equity ratio.

The presence of low or no debt in some of the SLPEs, especially in the utility and the co-operative sector enterprises, points to the total dependence of these enterprises on the GoS and also lack of sensitization on the part of both the GoS and the management of the SLPEs about the corporate financial management and linkages with the financial and capital markets.

Table 2.5: Debt-Equity Ratio

Name of the Enterprises	*2001-02*	*2002-03*	*2003-04*
SIDICO	0.21	0.18	0.15
State Bank of Sikkim	6.86	7.59	8.31
Sikkim State Co-operative Bank	0.00	0.00	0.00
Sikkim Jewels Ltd	0.29	0.31	0.08
Sikkim Hatchery Ltd	0.00	0.00	0.00
Sikkim Poultry Dev. Corp. Ltd	0.00	0.00	0.00
Sikkim Precision Industries	0.00	0.00	0.00
SITCO	0.09	0.07	0.05
Tea Board of Sikkim	0.00	0.00	0.00
Sikkim Milk Union	4.00	1.33	1.33
Govt. Fruit Preservation Factory	0.00	0.00	0.00
Sikkim Tourism Dev. Corp. Ltd	0.00	0.00	0.00
Sikkim Handloom and Handicrafts Dev. Corp. Ltd	0.00	0.00	0.00
Khadi and Village Industries Board	0.00	0.00	0.00
State Trading Corp. Ltd	0.00	0.00	0.00
Sikkim Consumer Co-operative Society	0.00	0.00	0.00
SIMFED	0.19	0.20	0.00
Denjong Agricultural Co-Operative Society Ltd	0.00	0.00	0.00
Sikkim Nationalized Transport Corp.	0.00	0.00	0.00
State Energy and Department of Power	0.00	0.00	0.00
Sikkim Power Dev. Corp.	16.67	16.67	16.67
SABCCO	1.41	1.24	1.25

Source: Computed on the basis of information contained in Annexures 1.1,1.2 and 1.3.

2.7 Profit Earning and Profitability

The SLPEs have to discharge both the 'public' and 'enterprise' roles. The 'enterprise' element should overtake the 'public' element with the accumulation of experience. The financial performance of the SLPEs as shown in Annexures 1.1 through 1.3 is summarized as under:

- The total accumulated losses wiped out 16.50 per cent of the total investments in the SLPEs in 2003-04. The provisioning for NPAs (Non-Performing Assets) by the State Bank of Sikkim and the accumulated losses incurred by SIDICO were mainly responsible for this phenomenon.
- In 2003-04 the net profit earned by the profit making enterprises was Rs 2.10 crore against the investment of Rs 124.01 crore giving a yield of 1.69er cent. The losses incurred by the loss making enterprises were Rs 34.84 crore

on an investment of Rs. 602.05 crore giving a negative yield of 5.78 per cent. On the whole the SLPEs earned a net loss of Rs. 32.74 crore on an investment of 726.06 crore resulting in a negative yield of 4.51 per cent.

- The net worth of the enterprises was about 11 per cent of the money invested in 2003-04.
- The capital employed also suffered a substantial erosion and amounted to a paltry 11.78 per cent of the total investment in 2003-04.

The profit earning record of the SLPEs as depicted in Anneuxres 1.1, 1.2 and 1.3 has been very dismal. The manufacturing, promotional, utility and welfare sector enterprises were, on the whole, in the red. The financial enterprise had a mixed fortune. The State Bank of Sikkim was deep in the red and in the case of the other financial enterprise the stated profits can not be taken at the face value as they carry huge contingent liabilities, sub-standard assets and doubtful debts. The trade and service enterprises excepting the Denjong Agricultural Co-operative Society managed to keep their head above water all due to protected market conditions. That the financial health of the SLPEs was not in pink is confirmed by the data on net worth which for all the enterprises taken together was an insignificant sum of Rs. 63.48 crore in 2003-04 as against the total investment of Rs. 726.06 crore during the same year. The financial laxity was rampant as seen by the relationship between the investment and capital employed. The total capital employed was Rs. 85.62 crore in 2003-04 as opposed to the total investment of Rs. 726.06 crore. This was a clear case of heavy capital erosion.

Table 2.6 reveals net profit/loss to total investment ratio for the SLPEs. It is clear that the SLPEs taken as a whole were in the red during all the three years of the study. However, the percentage of net losses to total investments declined during the period under reference due to reduction in losses incurred by State Bank of Sikkim and State Energy and Department of Power. The benchmark profitability as suggested by the Twelfth Finance Commission varies from two to five per cent on total investment for different categories of the SLPEs indicating the fact that the net profit to total investment ratio needed immediate attention and policy palliatives.

Table 2.6: Net Profit/Loss to Total Investments

Name of the Enterprises	*2001-02*	*2002-03*	*2003-04*
SIDICO	0.77	12.89	2.34
State Bank of Sikkim	–40.57	–433.13	–17.59
Sikkim State Co-operative Bank	12.82	2.58	7.37
Sikkim Jewels	–0.85	0.64	–5.40
Sikkim Hatchery	0.00	0.00	0.00
Sikkim Poultry	–2.53	–13.92	–10.13
Sikkim Precision Industries	0.00	3.24	1.08
SITCO	–4.26	–22.28	–28.02
Tea Board of Sikkim	0.41	–1.08	0.13
Sikkim Milk Union	–750.00	–507.14	–735.71
Govt. Fruit Preservation Factory	0.00	0.00	0.00
Sikkim Tourism	13.99	–20.04	–10.56
Sikkim Handloom and Handicrafts Dev. Corp	0.00	0.00	0.00
Khadi and Village Board	–2.08	–1.69	0.00
State Trading Corp.	67.57	0.00	59.46
Sikkim Consumer Co-operative Society	5.29	58.82	4.71
SIMFED	30.48	14.85	18.63
Denjong	–210.00	–170.00	–230.00
Sikkim Nationalized Transport Corp.	–11.31	–14.15	–12.21
State Energy and Department of Power	–13.98	–7.93	–4.41
Sikkim Power Dev. Corp.	0.00	0.00	0.00
SABCCO	2.24	1.99	0.60
Total	**–10.55**	**–9.54**	**–4.34**

Source: Computed from Annexures 1.1, 1.2 and 1.3.

2.8 Resource Use

The data given in Annexures 1.1, 1.2 and 1.3 show the resource use scenario in the SLPEs of the State of Sikkim. It is clear that the resource use was very low registering a declining trend in 2003-04. It was 14.51 per cent, 14.54 per cent and 14.51 per cent in 2001-02, 2002-03 and 2003-04, respectively. This was lower than the national average. The SLPEs pose a tremendous challenge for unlocking the hidden value. The manufacturing enterprises are a case in point. Sikkim Jewels Ltd., SITCO and Sikkim Precision Industries Ltd have been hardly using the capacity created and tapping the market for selling their goods. The power sector and transport sector enterprises are also characterized by low resource use.

2.9 Summing Up

The SLPEs system, inherited from the erstwhile Chogyal State, has continued to grow in the post integration era in Sikkim. A number of enterprises were set up in 1990s. The manufacturing enterprises dominated in terms of numbers whereas the utility enterprises had a substantial chunk of investments. Although the government company form turned out to be most popular, it could not yield the desired advantage as the State of Sikkim continue to uphold the validity of the Registration of Companies Act enacted by Chogyal in 1961. The investments in the SLPEs show that little respect was given to capital structuring as the debt-equity ratio was very low. A large number of enterprises exhibited their sole dependence on the State Government to obtain the equity support. Both the State Government and CEOs of the SLPEs did not appreciate the significance of linkages with the capital markets and the financial institutions. The profitability and the net worth turned out to be negative pointing to the heavy erosion of the capital base. The enterprises were overstaffed. There were too many non-managerial personnel comprising casual, work-charged and muster roll employees. The value added per employee and the average turnover per employee were insignificant. The resource use was abysmally low. The financial, and trading and service enterprises performed comparatively better. However, even in their case, the financial results can not be accepted at the face value due to the presence of sub-standard and doubtful assets, contingent liabilities and weak professional management.

The SLPEs scenario in the State of Sikkim points to the need of a re-look at the SLPEs portfolio to be retained by the Government and assess the scope for privatisation and disinvestment in the case of the enterprises required to be off loaded. The public policy of the GoS and the approach to translate such policy into action.

3

Privatisation Policy of Government of Sikkim

3.1 Policy of Government of Sikkim (GoS) on Disinvestment/ Privatisation

By beading together the various policy pronouncements, it is possible to glean the public policy on the SLPEs in the State of Sikkim. This chapter deals with the rationale, objectives, benefits, criteria and procedure for disinvestment/privatisation as stated by the GoS.

3.1.1 Rationale

The public sector has played a laudable role in enabling the State to achieve the objective of self-reliance. However, the significantly changed economic environment that now prevails both in the state and the country makes it imperative for both the public sector and the private sector to become competitive. Learning from the State experience, especially over the last decade, it is evident that disinvestment in public sector enterprises is no longer a matter of choice, but an imperative. The prolonged fiscal hemorrhage from the majority of these enterprises cannot be sustained any longer. The disinvestment would insure the availability of resources for other purposes which are at present are being pumped into these enterprises without any return.

The public sector has played a vital role in the development of the economy of the State of Sikkim. However, the nature of this role cannot remain frozen to what it was conceived years ago—a time when the technological landscape, and the domestic and national economic environment were so very different. The private sector in the State has come of age, contributing substantially to the development programmes launched by the State. Therefore, both the public sector and private sectors need to be viewed as mutually complementary parts of the industrial sector. The private sector must assume greater public responsibilities just as the public sector needs to focus more on achieving results in a highly competitive market. Most of the public enterprises have accumulated huge losses. With public finances under intense pressure, the State Government is just not able to sustain them much longer. Accordingly, the State Government is compelled to embark on the programme of disinvestment.

There are many SLPEs, which are sick and not capable of being revived. The only remaining option is to close down these undertakings after providing an acceptable safety net for the employees and workers. The GoS, at the state level, proposes to pursue the policy of the Government of India with regard to public enterprises at the central level. Consistent with the endeavour of the Central Government, downsizing of excess manpower through suitable scheme like VRS (Voluntary Retirement Scheme) would be implemented in the current Five Year Plan. The entire proceeds from disinvestment/privatisation would be deployed in social sectors and retirement of public debt. The public sector has overgrown itself and their shortcomings have manifested in the shape of low capacity utilization and low efficiency due to over manning and poor work ethics, over capitalization due to substantial time and cost overruns, inability to innovate, take quick and timely decisions, large interference in decision making process etc.

Because of a heavy incidence of the current revenue expenditure on items such as interest payments, wages and salaries of the GoS employees and subsidies, the GoS is left hardly with any surplus for capital expenditure on social and physical infrastructure. While the GoS would like to spend on basic education, primary health and family welfare, large amount of resources are blocked in several SLPEs. Not only this, the continued existence of the SLPEs is forcing the GoS to commit further resources for the sustenance of many non-viable SLPEs. The GoS continues to expose the taxpayers' money to risk, which it can readily avoid. To top it all, there is a huge amount of debt overhang, which needs to be serviced and reduced before money is available to invest in infrastructure. All this makes disinvestment of the GoS stake in the SLPEs absolutely imperative.

In order to make the existing SLPEs and Corporations more competitive in this age of liberalization, appropriate fiscal measures would be initiated including disinvestment on the merits of each individual case. Consultancies would be engaged to decide the entire gamut of modernization, diversification, revival of viable sick units and disinvestment. However, the SLPEs provide employment to thousands of people. This social aspect many have to be taken into consideration in the small state like Sikkim while deciding the matter of disinvestment and adopting a cautious approach.

The rationale for restructuring the SLPEs in the State of Sikkim as expounded by the GoS may be summarized as under:

- The GoS accepts, by and large, the need for restructuring SLPEs in the era of economic liberalization paving the growth of private sector.
- The restructuring of the SLPEs would be decided on a case to case basis.
- The manpower in the SLPEs would be right sized through VRS.
- The social consequences of restructuring the SLPEs would be given due consideration in deciding about the portfolio of their retention with the GoS.

3.1.2 *Objective*

The major objectives for disinvesting/privatizing the SLPEs are as follows:

- Releasing large amount of public resources locked up in non-productive SLPEs, for redeployment in areas that are much higher on the social priority, such as, basic health, family welfare, primary education and social and essential infrastructure.
- Stemming further outflow of scarce public resources for sustaining the unviable SLPEs.
- Reducing the public debt that is threatening to assume unmanageable proportions.

- Transferring the commercial risk, to which the taxpayers' money locked up in the public sector is exposed, to the private sector wherever the private sector is willing and able to step in. The money that is deployed in the SLPEs is really the public money and is exposed to an entirely avoidable and needless risk, in most cases.
- Releasing other tangible and intangible resources, such as, large manpower currently locked up in managing the SLPEs, and their time and energy, for redeployment in high priority social sectors that are short of such resources.

The GoS is compelled to support restructuring of the SLPEs due to growing resource crunch and fiscal deficit. The disinvestment and privatisation of the SLPEs is being considered as good economics in the State.

3.1.3 Incidental Benefits

The GoS expects to harness the following incidental benefits from the disinvestment/privatisation of the SLPEs:

- Disinvestments would expose the privatised companies to market discipline, thereby forcing them to become more efficient and survive or cease on their own financial and economic strength. They would be able to respond to the market forces much faster and cater to their business needs in a more professional manner. It would also facilitate in freeing such companies from the GoS control and introduce corporate governance in the privatised companies.
- Disinvestments should result in wider distribution of wealth through offering of shares of privatised companies to small investors.
- The restructuring would provide access to the existing SLPEs to appropriate private investment and thereby increase economic activity and have an overall beneficial effect on the economy, employment and tax revenues in the medium to long term.
- The disinvestment would result in optimal use of resources and assets in the SLPEs by unleashing their inherent productive potential.

3.1.4 Preconditions and Criteria

The GoS proposes to ensure that disinvestment does not result in unwarranted alienation of state assets. Further, it does not propose to take any action that may result in formation of private monopolies. The criteria for disinvestment/privatisation are as follows:

- Government would disinvest/privatise public sector undertakings, which are making losses for the last three years.
- Government would disinvest/privatise public sector undertakings, which have not paid dividends to the Government of Sikkim for the last three years.
- Government would disinvest/Privatize public sector undertakings from which the return on investments is less than the prime-lending rate of the Nationalized Banks.

However, it is relevant to mention that excepting the State Trading Corporation and the Sikkim State Co-operative Bank, no other SLPEs declared dividends. Further, the dividends declared were far lower than the prime lending rate of the commercial banks. To add the returns on investments in the case of the profitable enterprises SLPEs were far lower than the prime lending rate of the Nationalised Banks. Whereas, seven enterprises continuously incurred losses during 2001-02 to 2003-04, only four enterprises continuously earned profits.

3.1.5 Procedure

The GoS proposes to follow the following procedure for disinvestment/privatisation to promote administrative simplicity and fasten the speed of decision-making without compromising on transparency and fair play:

- Proposals for disinvestment/privatization in any SLPE, based on the recommendations of the Administrative Department would be placed for consideration of the GoS through the Minister in charge of the concerned SLPE.
- The GoS clears the disinvestment proposal, the valuation of the assets of the SLPE would be done by the concerned

technical departments of GoS Sikkim. The value of the current assets so calculated will serve as the floor/reserve price for the purpose of bidding.

- The bidders would be invited through advertisement in newspapers/website to submit their Expression of Interest (EoI) in the first stage. After receipt of the Expression of Interest (EoI), in pursuance of Advertisement in newspapers/website, a list of bidders will be prepared.
- The bidders would be undertake due diligence of the SLPE and hold discussions with the Administrative Department/ the representatives of the SLPE for any clarifications.
- The bidders would be asked to submit their financial offers. Based on the highest offer received from the prospective bidders, the Sale Agreement/Lease Agreement will be finalised by the Administrative Department. After getting the Sale Agreement/Lease Agreement vetted by the Department of Law, the Sale Agreement will be approved by the Government.
- After the transaction is completed, copies of all papers and documents relating to the transaction would be sent to Finance Department of the State for reference and record.

3.2 Summing Up

Restructuring business enterprises is the order of the day. Restructuring effects suitable changes to align the current business practices in tune with the changed requirements. Restructuring brings about a long-term change and renders the business fit to match the changing business requirements. Restructuring includes in its gamut organizational, financial, human resource, operational and strategic re-alignment. The privatisation, disinvestment and closer constitute a part of such restructuring. The GoS has formulated a comprehensive policy with regard to privatisation and disinvestment. By and large, the GoS proposes to privatize/ disinvest the SLPEs which are not strategic in nature. It is expected that such disengagement would lead to the development of private sector and freeing resources which are unwarrantedly locked up in the public sector. The GoS proposes to carryout the entire restructuring exercise on case-to-case basis in a transparent manner without hurting the interest of workers. The SLPEs are encouraged to formulate their VRS to minimize the social consequences of labour adjustments. The GoS has also formulated some criteria for disinvestment to avoid subjectivity in the selection of candidates for disinvestment and pre-empt formation of monopolies. However, these criteria need an analytical formulation to identify the candidates for privatisation, disinvestment and retention. This alone could indicate as to what should be the SLPEs portfolio for retention by the GoS and as to which modality could be followed for privatisation/disinvestment of the left over SLPEs. This forms the subject matter of the next section. It is appropriate to mention here that such an analytical formulation would stand out as a superior proposition to the criteria indicated by the GoS in that besides considering profitability of the SLPEs, it considers their public purpose, resource mobilisation and market structure and also outlines modalities of restructuring and privatisation.

4

Scope and Modalities for Restructuring SLPEs

The purpose of this chapter is to discuss the models for identifying the candidates for disinvestment/privatisation and list out the SLPEs for disinvestment/privatisation and retention and evolves a framework for the modalities of restructuring and privatization of SLPEs in the State of Sikkim.

4.1 Conceptual Models

Figures 4.1 and 4.2 present the conceptual models that could suit the requirement for identifying the SLPEs in the State of Sikkim for the purposes of disinvestment, privatisation and retention. The first model is known as the Three Dimensional Matrix and the second one is know as the Two-by-Two Matrix.

4.1.1 Three Dimensional Matrix

The Three Dimensional Matrix based on factors such as: (1) public purpose, (2) mobilization of resources from external sources, and (3) profitability could be applied to rank public enterprises as high or low. The enterprises being high on all three dimensions merit retention in the public enterprise portfolio. On the other hand, the enterprises being low on all three dimensions need to be transferred to the private sector. The enterprises falling in intermediate categories need to undergo restructuring.

Factors	*High*	*Low*
1. Public Purpose	H1	L1
2. Resource Mobilisation from Financial Institutions	H2	L2
3. Profitability	H3	H3

Fig. 4.1: Three Dimensional Matrix

4.1.2 Two-by-Two Matrix

The second model is based on financial performance and market structure. The SLPEs may have a positive or negative financial performance. In terms of market structure, they may constitute a single source of supply or constitute to multiple sources of supply. The enterprises registering good financial performance and having multiple sources of supply emerge as clear candidates for privatization. On the contrary, the enterprises characterized with good financial performance but belonging to single source of supply need to be retained in the public enterprise portfolio. The SLPEs in the other categories need to be restructured.

<table>
<tr><td rowspan="6">Market Structure</td><td colspan="3">Financial Performance</td></tr>
<tr><td>Good</td><td></td><td>Bad</td></tr>
<tr><td>Single Source</td><td>A</td><td>B</td></tr>
<tr><td></td><td>Non-Competitive Successful PEs</td><td>Non-Competitive Unsuccessful PEs</td></tr>
<tr><td>Multiple Source</td><td>C</td><td>D</td></tr>
<tr><td></td><td>Competitive Successful PEs</td><td>Competitive Unsuccessful</td></tr>
</table>

Fig. 4.2: Two-by-Two Matrix

4.2 Identifying SLPEs for Restructuring

The data for the year 2003-04 pertaining to the SLPEs have been considered for the application of the three dimensional matrix and the Two-by-Two Matrix.

Public purpose is considered high if the enterprise is involved in core activities which can not be totally executed by the private sector. Resource mobilisation is considered high if 20 per cent or more of the resources have been raised externally. Profitability is considered high if the net profits earned are more than ten per cent of the investment.

Table 4.1: Three Dimensional Matrix and SLPEs

Name of the Enterprise	*Public Purpose**	*Resource Mobilization***	*Profitability****
SIDICO	High	High	Low
State Bank of Sikkim	High	High	Low
Sikkim State Co-operative Bank	High	Low	Low
Sikkim Jewels Ltd	Low	Low	Low
Sikkim Hatchery Ltd	Low	Low	Low
Sikkim Poultry	Low	Low	Low
Sikkim Precision Industries	Low	Low	Low
SITCO	Low	Low	Low
Tea Board of Sikkim	High	Low	Low
Sikkim Milk Union	High	High	Low
Govt. Fruit Preservation Factory	Low	Low	Low
Sikkim Tourism	High	Low	Low
Sikkim Handicrafts and Handlooms Development Corporation	High	Low	Low
Khadi and Village Industries Board	High	Low	Low
State Trading Corp.	Low	Low	High
Sikkim Consumer Co-operative	Low	Low	Low
Society SIMFED	High	Low	High
Denjong Agricultural Co-Operative Society Ltd	High	Low	High
Sikkim National Transport Corp.	High	Low	Low
State Energy and Department of Power	High	Low	Low
Sikkim Power Dev. Corp.	Low	Low	Low
SABCCO	High	High	Low

* The objectives of the enterprises are furnished in Annexure 1.4
** The resource mobilization scenario is given in Annexure 1.5
*** The profit performance is given in Annexure 1.6

As per the Three Dimensional Matrix, there is no SLPE in Sikkim qualifying for straight retention. However, there are nine SLPEs requiring privatisation/closure. These enterprises include Sikkim Jewels Ltd, Sikkim Hatchery Ltd, Sikkim Poultry Dev. Corp. Ltd, Sikkim Precision Dev. Corp. Ltd, Sikkim Time Corp., Sikkim Trading Corp., Sikkim State Consumer Co-operative Society, Government Fruit Preservation Factory, and Sikkim Power Dev. Corp. Ltd. Though Sikkim Consumer Co-operative Society and State Trading Corp. have been profit making ventures, their privatisation/winding up has been suggested in view of the duplication of activities with SIMFED and the Denjong Agricultural Co-operative Society as discussed later in section 8.20. The rest of the enterprises (namely, SIDICO, State Bank of Sikkim, Sikkim State Consumer Co-operative Bank, Tea Board of Sikkim, Sikkim Milk Producers Union, Sikkim Tourism Dev. Corp. Ltd., Sikkim Handloom and Handicrafts Dev. Corp. Ltd, Khadi and Village Industries Board, SIMFED, Denjong Agricultural Society, Sikkim Nationalized Transport, Sikkim Energy and Department of Power and SABCCO) need to be restructured as per the suitably designed modalities.

		Competitive	*Non-Competitive*
Financial Performance	Profit Making	1. Sikkim Precision Industries Ltd. 2. State Trading Corporation 3. Government Fruit Preservation Factory	1. Sikkim Industrial and Investment Development Corporation Ltd. 2. Sikkim State Co-operative Bank 3. Tea Board of Sikkim 4. Sikkim Consumers' Co-operative Society 5. Sikkim State Co-operative Supply and Marketing Federation Ltd.
		First Quadrant	**Second Quadrant**
	Loss Making	1. Sikkim Jewels Ltd. 2. Sikkim Hatchery Ltd. 3. Sikkim Poultry Dev. Corp. Ltd. 4. Sikkim Times Corp. Ltd. 5. Sikkim Co-operative Milk Producers Union Ltd. 6. Sikkim Power Dev. Corp.	1. State Bank of Sikkim 2. Sikkim Tourism Development Corporation Ltd. 3. Sikkim Nationalized Transport 4. Sikkim State Energy and Power Department 5. Sikkim Handloom and Handicrafts Dev. Corp. Ltd. 6. Khadi and Village Industries Board 7. Denjong Agricultural Co-Operative Society Ltd. 8. Sikkim Scheduled Castes, Tribes and Other Backward Classes Development Corporation Ltd.
		Third Quadrant	**Fourth Quadrant**
		Same as first Quadrant	Same as second quadrant

Fig. 4.3: Two-by-Two Matrix and SLPEs

Figure 4.3 shows that three enterprise viz., Sikkim Precision Industries Ltd, State Trading Corporation and Government Fruit Preservation Factory qualify for privatisation as they are profitable and are also competitive. The table shows that five enterprises, viz Sikkim Industrial and Investment Development Corporation Ltd, Sikkim State Co-operative Bank, Tea Board of Sikkim, Sikkim Consumers' Co-operative Society, and Sikkim State Co-operative Supply and Marketing Federation Ltd. are profitable but non-competitive. These enterprises need to be made competitive and in course of time required to be shifted to the first Quadrant making them amenable, if necessary, for privatisation. There is a need to introduce policy and managerial reforms to shift these enterprises to the first quadrant. Quadrant three shows viz., Sikkim Jewels Ltd, Sikkim Hatchery Ltd, Sikkim Poultry Dev. Corp. Ltd, Sikkim Times Corp. Ltd, Sikkim Co-operative Milk Producers Union Ltd and Sikkim Power Dev. Corp. There is a need to introduce policy and managerial reforms to shift these enterprises to the first Quadrant. Quadrant four shows that eight enterprises viz., State Bank of Sikkim, Sikkim Tourism Development Corporation Ltd, Sikkim Nationalized Transport, Sikkim State Energy and Power Department, Sikkim Handloom and Handicrafts Dev. Corp. Ltd, Khadi and Village Industries Board, Denjong Agricultural Co-Operative Society Ltd, and Sikkim Scheduled Castes, Tribes and Other Backward Classes Development Corporation Ltd. are loss making and non-competitive. There is a need to make these enterprises competitive and then introduce managerial reforms in order to shift them from Quadrant four to Quadrant three and eventually to Quadrant one.

The application of the two models provides the same choice for the portfolio for retention of the SLPEs in the State of Sikkim which facilitates our task of outlining the modalities for restructuring and privatisation.

4.3 Modalities of Restructuring

The SLPEs are ranked as high or low on various parameters of the three dimensional matrix. By placing them on the three dimensional matrix, we obtained 2x2x2 i.e. 8 categories containing 22 enterprises. No enterprise was high on all the parameters. Eight enterprises were low on all the parameters. 14 enterprises belonged to the other six categories. The State Trading Corporation has also been identified for privatisation/closure due to its presence in non-strategic area of operation. Table 4.2 provides the details in terms three dimensional matrix of category-wise listing of the SLPEs in the State of Sikkim.

Table 4.2: Categorization of SLPEs as per Three Dimensional Matrix

Category Name	*Name of the Enterprise*
Category 1: Public purpose high, resource mobilization high, profitability high	#
Category 2: Public purpose low, resource mobilization low, profitability low	• Sikkim Jewels Ltd • Sikkim Hatchery Ltd • Sikkim Poultry • Sikkim Precision Industries • SITCO • Govt. Fruit Preservation Factory • Sikkim Consumer Co-operative society • Sikkim Power Dev. Corp.
Category 3: Public purpose high, resource mobilization low, and profitability low	• Sikkim State Co-operative Bank • Tea Board of Sikkim • Sikkim Tourism • Sikkim Handicrafts and Handlooms Development Corporation • Khadi and Village Industries Board • Sikkim National Transport Corp. • State Energy and Department of Power
Category 4: Public purpose high, resource mobilization low, profitability high:	• SIMFED • Denjong Agricultural Co-Operative Society Ltd
Category 5: Public purpose high, resource mobilization high, profitability low	• SIDICO • State Bank of Sikkim • Sikkim Milk Union • SABCCO
Category 6: Public purpose low, resource mobilization high, profitability low	#
Category 7: Public purpose low, resource mobilization low, profitability high	• State Trading Corporation
Category 8: Public purpose low, resource mobilization high, profitability high	#

No enterprise classified in this category.

The modalities for restructuring category-wise are discussed below:

Category 1

Public purpose high, resource mobilization high, profitability high: The SLPEs in this category should be continued since they are good performers. They should be freed from government control on operational issue matters. The Memorandum of Understanding (MoU) should specify support to be extended and financial returns expected by the Government. The Governing Boards of these enterprises should not have more than one government nominees. All measures under cold privatisation could be adopted for enterprises in this category. The enterprises in this category should be provided autonomy and become financially viable. The term cold privatisation refers to optimum performance through internal management action which calls for introduction and strengthening of financial and management systems such as budgeting, costing, pricing, internal audit, manpower planning, recruitment, performance appraisal, training and management development, supply chain management, technological up-gradation, computerisation and restructuring of varied kinds, viz., organisational, financial, human resources, operations and technological restructuring. No SLPE has been ranked as high-high-high.

Category 2

Public performance low, resource mobilization low, profitability low: The enterprises in this category are a fit case for liquidation or total divesture, if possible. This would lead to avoidance of further investment thereby reducing the burden on the State exchequer. Sikkim Jewels Ltd, Sikkim Hatchery Ltd, Sikkim Poultry Ltd, Sikkim Precision Industries, SITCO, Govt. Fruit Preservation Factory, Sikkim Consumer Co-operative Society and Sikkim Power Dev. Corp. come in this category of the three dimensional matrix.

Category 3

Public purpose high, resource mobilization low, and profitability low: These enterprises should be continued in the state sector. The accent on resource mobilization and profitability should be increased and then partial/cold privatization could be attempted. Sikkim State Co-operative Bank, Tea Board of Sikkim, Sikkim Tourism Dev. Corp. Ltd, Sikkim Handicrafts and Handlooms Development Corp., Khadi and Village Industries Board, Sikkim National Transport Corp., State Energy and Department of Power, form a part of this category.

Category 4

Public purpose high, resource mobilization low, profitability high: The enterprises in this category could be continued in the State sector. The accent should be on improving the resource mobilization increased borrowings on commercial terms. The profitability improvement measures could also be introduced to improve the market standing of the enterprises. The enterprises in this category then be partially privatized. SIMFED and Denjong Agricultural Co-Operative Society Ltd., form a part of this category as enterprises.

Category 5

Public purpose high, resource mobilization high, profitability low: While enterprises in this category could be continued in the State sector, there should be total reorganization of internal management and profitability elements concerning these enterprises. SIDICO, State Bank of Sikkim, SABCCO and Sikkim Milk Union form a part of this category of enterprises.

Category 6

Public purpose low, resource mobilization high, profitability low: Such cases should go in for disinvestment. Total divestiture could also be attempted. Although, no enterprise falls in this category, any enterprise established in future, qualifying for this category, should be taken up for disinvestment or total divestiture.

Category 7

Public purpose low, resource mobilization low, profitability high: In such cases the government fund could be withdrawn by borrowing more from the market and institutions in view of the good profitability. The enterprises in this category could be considered initially for partial divestiture leading to full divestiture in the final course. State Trading Corporation is the cases in point concerning this category.

Category 8

Public purpose low, resource mobilization high, and profitability high: These form appropriate cases for total disinvestment resulting in capital accretions for the State government. No SLPE qualifies for inclusion in this category.

The anticipated benefits of the modalities suggested are given in Table 4.3.

4.4 Privatisation Method

An enterprise could be privatised with or without divestiture. The divestiture could be full or partial. The privatisation without divestiture could be positive or negative. The choice of methods would be determined by the characteristics possessed by each enterprise in terms of being strategic or non-strategic in nature. Both the strategic and non-strategic enterprises creating fiscal pressures by continued loss making need to be removed from the portfolio for retention of the SLPEs. However, between the strategic and non-strategic enterprises, it is easier to privatise the non-strategic enterprises.

4.5 Requirement for Restructuring

In order to affect restructuring for privatisation, disinvestment and retention, some legal, accounting and financial requirements need to be fulfilled besides pledging the political commitment. The legal requirements include the settlement of claims of employees, fulfilment of the provisions of the companies act and corporatisation of the departmental enterprises. The accounting requirements comprise the updation of accounts, assessment of contingent liabilities and settlement of claims. The financial requirements include the changes in the debt-equity ratio, broadening of capital structure, introduction of financial systems

Table 4.3: Anticipated Benefits of Modalities

Categorization of SLPEs			*Names of SLPEs and No. of SLPEs*	*Suggested Action*	*Anticipated Results*
Public Purpose	*Resource mobilization*	*Profit ability*			
H1	H2	H3	#	Continue in the state sector with greater autonomy	Better service to consumers
L1	L2	L3	• Sikkim Jewels Ltd. • Sikkim Hatchery Ltd • Sikkim Poultry Ltd • Sikkim Precisions Industries Ltd • SITCO • Govt. Fruit Preservation Factory • Sikkim Consumer Co-operative Society • Sikkim Power Development Corp. Ltd	Closure or Liquidation or total divestiture	Saving of Govt. Resources
H2	L2	L3	• Sikkim State Co-operative Bank • Tea Board of Sikkim • Sikkim Tourism Dev. Corp. Ltd • Sikkim Handicrafts and Handloom Dev. Corp. Ltd • Khadi and Village Industries Board	Continue in the state sector with increased accent on resource mobilisation and profitability	Improved fulfilment of public purpose

(Contd)

(Contd)

Categorization of SLPEs			Names of SLPEs and No. of SLPEs	Suggested Action	Anticipated Results
Public Purpose	Resource mobilization	Profit ability			
H1	L2	H3	• Sikkim National Transport Corp. • State Energy and Department of Power • SIMFED • Denjong Agricultural Co-operative Society Ltd	Increased accent on the resource mobilisation/ partial disinvestment	Better Revenues or reduced budget support
H1	H2	L3	• SIDICO • State Bank of Sikkim • Sikkim Milk Producers Union • SABCCO	Disinvest	Additional resource to Govt.
L1	H2	L3	#	Introduce financial adjustments and then go in for disinvestment	Long-term Improvement in service to consumers
L1	L2	H3	• State Trading Corp. Ltd	Introduce financial adjustments and then go in for disinvestment	Long-term Investment in service to consumers
L1	H2	H3	#	Disinvest	Reduced Govt. support

#No enterprise classified in this category

and valuation of the enterprise. The socio-political requirements include the creation of pro-restructuring/privatisation climate, transparency in restructuring/privatisation, setting up independent machinery for the purpose and strong political commitment ensuring the successful functioning of the post-privatised enterprises. The setting up of regulatory bodies, wherever required, is also necessary for the success.

4.6 Characteristics of SLPEs in the State of Sikkim

Annexure 1.7 throws light on the characteristics relating to the activities, financial status, physical performance, total employment, social purpose, financial system and management, interface with government, performance improvement plan, SWOT analysis, problems encountered, and strategic initiatives. The following generalizations emerge from Annexure 1.7:

- A majority of the enterprises have been incorporated in the company form. All the manufacturing enterprises excepting Sikkim Co-operative Milk Union have been registered as the Government Company. The social purpose of these enterprises (excepting Sikkim Co-operative Milk Union) is very low. They qualify for full privatisation. The Sikkim Power Development Corporation, although an enterprise in the utility category, has also a low social purpose and qualifies for full privatisation. SABCCO and Sikkim Tourism Development Corporation have a high social purpose. In their cases, cold privatisation could be introduced through Optimum Performance Through Internal Management Action (OPTIMA).
- The utility enterprises are large sized. They operate as departmental enterprises. There is a need to corporatise these enterprises, make them competitive, and commercially and financially viable. Partial/full privitisation could follow thereafter.
- Out of four public corporations, two corporations, viz., State Bank of Sikkim, Khadi and Village Industries Board, and Tea Board of Sikkim have a high public purpose, and State Trading Corporation has a low public purpose.

Whereas, the first three need to be retained in the public sector, the last one needs to be privatized. However, in both the cases, partial/full privatisation or cold privatisation could be considered as per the need of each case.

- In the case of co-operative enterprises, public purpose being high, the retention is the only option presently available with the government. However, in their case also, there is a possibility of merger and OPTIMA
- The size of the SLPEs in the State of Sikkim is small in terms of both the turnover and the volume. This makes them amenable for restructuring and privatisation.
- The financial position of the enterprises is very discouraging as most of the enterprises completely depend for share capital on the government, have not garnered debt, are characterized by receding or negative net worth due to accumulated losses, and are incurring losses. Some of the enterprises have either low or negative working capital.
- The wage costs are very high as non-managerial staff far exceeds the managerial staff in number. The overstaffing has taken place through the muster roll, work-charged and casual employment routes. Some enterprises have tried to go in for labour adjustments through VRS but the success has been minimal and a lot more remains to be done.
- The revenues earned/turnover of the enterprises is very low and is about 15 per cent of the total investment. The capacity utilisation in manufacturing enterprises ranges from 10 to 30 per cent.
- The enterprises have perennially continued with same activities without any R&D and innovations.
- The financial and management systems such as budgeting, costing, pricing, internal audit, management information system (MIS), project appraisal, recruitment, manpower planning, supply chain management, appointment of professional directors, excessive presence of government directors on the board have encouraged non commercial culture and bureaucratisation. The enterprises are not board-led ones.

- The SWOT analysis points that strengths are far less as compared to weaknesses and so is the case between opportunities and threats.
- Most of the enterprise did not formulate performance improvement plans and are not internally funded. Further, many enterprises lack the government support in that there interaction with government is very low.
- The problems faced by these enterprises are galore ranging from operations related, market mix, location, over aging of plant and machinery to strategic issues such as settlement of debts, diversification, finding new markets, innovating new sources of finance, increase in employee productivity, unwarranted internal competition and neglect of technology, to mention a few.
- The SLPEs have shown a very poor appreciation for strategic initiatives including the rationalization of manpower and modernization of plant and machinery. The issues in organisaitonal, financial, human resource development and industrial relations, operational and technological restructuring have not been attended to by them.

4.7 Summing Up

The application of the restructuring models clearly point out a vast scope for policy and managerial reforms for the SLPEs that are required to be retained in the medium and long-term by the GoS and privatisation/disinvestment of un-strategic SLPEs. The modalities with regard to the privatisation of these enterprise and the restructuring packages for privatisation/disinvestment and managerial reforms are discussed in next chapter.

5

Restructuring Plans

5.1 Restructuring Plans

The need for restructuring the SLPEs is amply demonstrated by Table 5.1. The investments in the SLPEs have become unproductive and cost the GoS Rs. 190.52 crore in 2003-04. This is a huge sum. The returns were negative also in the years 2001-02 and 2002-03. The GoS must unlock the value hidden in the SLPEs. The restructuring of loans obtained by SABCCO, Sikkim Power Development Ltd, and Sikkim Time Corporation Ltd would brighten the profit and loss accounts and balance sheets of these enterprises and also reduce the risk for the GoS.

Table 5.1: Cost and Returns from Investments in SLPEs

(Rs. in crore)

	Particulars	*2001-02*	*2002-03*	*2003-04*
1.	Total Investment	663.34	676.86	726.06
2.	Opportunity Cost (@ 10 % on Total Investment)	66.33	67.68	72.61
3.	Add Net loss	72.75	66.06	32.74
4.	Add Subsidies*	0.86	3.81	0.84
5.	**Total (2+3+4)**	139.94	137.55	106.19
6.	*Less* Dividends	0.14	0	0.01
7.	**Gross Direct Cost (5-6)**	139.80	137.55	106.18
8.	Add Guarantees	95.89	86.19	84.34
9.	**Total Cost (7+8)**	**235.69**	**223.74**	**190.52**

**Source*: Annexure 1.8.

5.2 Macro and Micro Restructuring Plans

In this section, an attempt has been made to provide the macro and the micro restructuring plans related to the SLPEs. It is important to note in this context that the SLPEs have been set up as an instrument of public policy by the GoS. Further, Sikkim is relatively a new State in the north-east. Therefore, any move about restructuring/privatisation has to be considered in the backdrop of the fact that in the present phase of economic development of the State, some SLPEs would continue to play an important role. To add, these enterprises are the only source of organized employment in Sikkim outside the government structure. The restructuring plans formulated are based on the financial data pertaining to March 31, 2004.

5.2.1 Macro Approach to Restructuring

There is a need to formulate some broad principles for restructuring which could be pursued by the GoS to tackle issues relating to the SLPEs. These broad principles could be formulated on the basis of an intensive study of the functioning and performance of these enterprises.

A study of the objectives (*See: Annexure 1.4*) and the profile (*See: Annexure 1.7*) of these enterprises very clearly reveal the duplication of activities in the case of Sikkim Consumer Co-operative Society, the Denjong Agricultural Co-operative Society, Sikkim State Co-operative Supply and Marketing Federation and State Trading Corporation. All these enterprises are engaged in the activities of procurement of goods and supply of services to the government departments. These enterprises operate on a margin which provides them a spread adequate enough to cover the costs over a period of time. These enterprises solely depend on procurements and have not been developing new business. The procurement costs of these enterprises are increasing. On the part of these enterprises, the problem of delayed payment or non-payment from the government departments is becoming more and more acute. Further, the user enterprises and the government departments have been complaining about the delays in supply and also excessive costs. *It is suggested that State Trading Corp. Ltd and Sikkim Consumer Co-operative Society be privatised/wound-up as they are involved in non-core business activity.*

The State should not set up any enterprise in future intended to take up a non-core activity. A non-core activity is an activity that serves low social purpose which can be taken up by the private sector on the grounds of its presence and suitability.

There are some enterprises serving high social purpose but involved in the conduct of partly non-core activities. These enterprises comprise the Denjong Agricultural Co-operative Society, Sikkim State Co-operative Supply and Marketing Federation and Sikkim Handloom and Handicrafts Dev. Corp. Ltd. The Denjong Agricultural Co-operative Society and Sikkim State Co-operative Supply and Marketing Federation work under the same government department, serve the same clientele and duplicate some activities. The Denjong Agricultural Co-operative Society and Sikkim State Co-operative Supply and Marketing Federation need to be merged to avoid the duplication. The merged enterprise should refrain from undertaking the procurement business and concentrate on the core activity of serving its shareholders. The Sikkim Handloom and Handicraft Dev. Corp. Ltd should also concentrate on promotional activities and reduce its direct involvement in sale or manufacturing of handloom and handicrafts items.

All the manufacturing enterprises (excepting Sikkim Co-operative Milk Producers Union and Tea Board of Sikkim) have been found low on public purpose, resource mobilisation and profitability. These consist of Sikkim Jewels Ltd, Sikkim Hatchery Ltd, Sikkim Poultry Dev. Corp. Ltd, Sikkim Precision Industries, Govt. Fruit Preservation Factory and Sikkim Time Corporation. Sikkim Power Dev. Corp., a utility sector enterprise, has also been found low on public purpose, resource mobilisation and profitability. These enterprises are defunct for several years. These enterprises operate in a highly competitive market. The private sector is emerging as a strong player in the areas in which these enterprises operate. Not only that these enterprises have lost their market penetration but they have also lost their marketing muscle in terms of advertising and publicity. There is a need to privatise/ wind up all these enterprises. The GoS should weigh the objectives of setting up a proposed SLPE in terms of these indicators and if the answer is not in affirmative, the GoS should not set up such an enterprise in the state sector.

The utility sector enterprises viz., Sikkim Nationalized

Transport and Sikkim Energy and Department of Power form the lifeline of the State and need therefore to be retained in the public sector. However, their corporatisation is necessary. Once they are corporatised, OPTIMA could be introduced in these enterprises.

The welfare and promotional enterprises have to be continued in the state sector as they deal with the up-liftment of the down trodden classes of society and development of certain economic activity. It is in this backdrop that SABCCO, Khadi and Village Industries Board and Sikkim Tourism Dev. Corp. could be retained in the portfolio of public sector by the GoS.

The financial enterprises such as SIDICO, State Bank of Sikkim and Sikkim State Co-operative Bank provide financial input for the economic development. They have high social purpose. However, their resource mobilisation and profitability are low. There internal management is very poor. They suffer from asset-liability mismatch. They have also watered assets. All this suggests that while they could continue in the public sector, they need to vigorously pursue OPTIMA and also enhance the size and volume of their operations.

To summarise, in the light of the suggestions with regard to the restructuring of the SLPEs their proposed status is discussed in Table 5.2.

The SLPEs in Sikkim are small sized entities in terms of investment, assets and turnover, innovations. They are loss making. The financial and management systems are conspicuous by their absences in these enterprises. The government control and direction relating to SLPEs in Sikkim is lacking in several regards. Although an official of the level of the Director in the Finance Department has been made responsible for coordinating the enterprise-government interface, he is saddled with several responsibilities and finds no time to attend to the issues relating to the SLPEs. In case finance department has surplus officials (or it could seek the services of an official from other departments who have surplus officials), *it is suggested to designate one such official as the Director (SLPEs) charged with the responsibility of inter-departmental coordination, preparation of an annual survey on the SLPEs, formulation of management development and training plans, clearing the arrears of annual accounts and reports in the SLPEs by extending support in terms of accounting personnel and providing guidelines on the wage and performance evaluation matters. Such an official should also have some exposure on public enterprise reforms carried out in some countries and states in India such as Andhra Pradesh, Karnataka, Orissa and West Bengal.*

Table 5.2: Suggested Status of SLPEs

Name of the Enterprises	*To be Retained*	*To be Merged*	*To be Privatised/ wound up*
Sikkim Industrial and Investment Development Corporation Ltd	*		
State Bank of Sikkim	*		
Sikkim State Co-operative Bank	*		
Sikkim Jewels			*
Sikkim Hatchery			*
Sikkim Poultry			*
Sikkim Precision Industries			*
Sikkim Time Company			*
Tea Board of Sikkim	*		
Govt. Fruit Preservation Factory			*
Sikkim Co-operative Milk Producers Union Ltd	*		
Sikkim Tourism	*		
Sikkim Handloom and Handicrafts Development Corp. Ltd	*		
Khadi and Village Industries Board	*		
State Trading Corp.			*
Sikkim Consumer Co-operative Society			*
Sikkim State Co-operative Supply and Marketing Federation Ltd		*	
Denjong Agricultural Co-Operative Society Ltd		*	
Sikkim Nationalized Transport Corp.	*		
State Energy and Department of Power	*		
Sikkim Power Dev. Corp.			*
SABCCO	*		
Total	**11**	**2**	**9**

The Director (SLPEs) should immediately look into the problems of manpower planning, wage policies, internal audit and control systems in the SLPEs. Almost all the enterprises do not have any sensitization about management development and training in that generally employees are not exposed to training and management development, and no in-house training programmes are organized by the SLPEs. The CEOs of the SLPEs hardly interact with policy makers. At the most, some enterprises interact twice or thrice with the policy makers. Table 5.3 reveals the quality of interaction in the SLPEs.

Table 5.3 shows that 12 enterprises had low or very low interface with the GoS. Only three enterprises had high interface. Seven enterprises had moderate interface. The lack of interface obstructed quick disposal of files, resulted in delays in sorting out problematic issues and did not nurture the requisite trust between the enterprises and the GoS.

Table 5.3: Quality of Interface with the GoS

Name of the SLPEs	*Quality of Interface*
SIDICO	Moderate
State Bank of Sikkim	High
Sikkim State Co-operative Bank	Moderate
Sikkim Jewels	Low
Sikkim Hatchery	Very Low
Sikkim Poultry	Very Low
Sikkim Precision Industries	Very Low
SITCO	Very Low
Tea Board of Sikkim	Very Low
Sikkim Milk Union	Moderate
Govt. Fruit Preservation Factory	Low
Sikkim Tourism	Very High
Sikkim Handloom and Handicrafts Dev. Corp. Ltd	Moderate
Khadi and Village Board	Low
State Trading Corp.	Low
Sikkim Consumer Co-operative Society	Moderate
SIMFED	Low
Denjong	Low
Sikkim National Transport Corp.	Moderate
State Energy and Department of Power	Very High
Sikkim Power Dev. Corp.	Low
SABCCO	Moderate

H—High, M—Moderate and L—Low
Source: Annexure 1.7.

The annual accounts are in arrears in a number of cases and the quality of disclosure is very poor. The absence of professionals at the middle level has hit hard the functioning of these enterprises. The Director (SLPEs) could hire the services of charted accountants, cost accountants, company secretaries and lawyers to institute effective accounting systems in the SLPEs and clear the arrears of accounts. The project evaluation and project management skills are also lacking in the SLPEs. The Director (SLPEs), could organize these services and extend them to these enterprises. It is worth mentioning that some enterprises have undertaken large investments in plant and machinery to manufacture new products without proper project evaluation and effective implementation. Such projects have vitiated the entire project economics of some SLPEs and pushed them in the red. The Director (SLPEs) should also look into the legal framework governing the SLPEs. For instance, the laws governing the SLPEs should be integrated with the laws of the main land. In this connection, it is appropriate to mention that the Registration of Companies Act of Sikkim and the Income Tax Act of Sikkim should be immediately replaced by the Indian Companies Act and the Indian Income Tax Act. This, among other things, will facilitate better corporate governance and access to export incentives to the SLPEs in Sikkim. *It is suggested that the Director (SLPEs) may formulate an agenda for action for effective exercise of the government control, on the one hand, and provide strategic assistance to the SLPEs, on the other. He should refrain from becoming the fifth wheel in the coach.*

The successful functioning of an enterprise depends on the composition of its board and the autonomy provided to it by the government. It has been found that most of the boards of the SLPEs are packed with the government nominees and that the board decisions get referred finally to the government Table 5.4 shows the compositions of the boards of the SLPEs. *It is suggested that the board composition should be balanced with the representation of professional directors, user interests, employee representatives, and the government nominees. The strength of the board should be between seven and twelve depending on the size of the organisations. The government nominees should not exceed a number of more than two at the maximum. The position of managing director and chairman could be combined to cut the red tape, quicken the decision making and curb infructuous expenses. It has been observed that the separation of the post of chairman-cum-managing director has resulted in wasteful expenditure and unhealthy organisational culture.*

Table 5.4: Board Composition

Name of the Enterprise	*Govt. Nominees (including nominees of financial institutions)*	*Functional Director*	*Independent Directors (Professionals)*	*Worker Nominee*	*Share holders*	*Other*	*Total*
SIDICO	7						7
State Bank of Sikkim	6						6
Sikkim State Co-operative Bank	6						6
Sikkim Jewels	6						6
Sikkim Poultry	1		1			6	8
SITCO	5	1					6
Tea Board of Sikkim							
Sikkim Milk Producers Union	5	2		8			15
Govt. Fruit Preservation Factory							
Sikkim Tourism	8			2			10
Sikkim Handloom and Handicrafts Dev. Corp. Ltd	1						8
Khadi and Village Board	11						11
State Trading Corp.	6						6
Sikkim Consumer Co-operative Soceity	5				4		9
SIMFED	5	4	1				10
Denjong Agricultural Co-operative Society	5		4				9
Sikkim Nationalized Transport Corp.			Departmental Enterprises				
State Energy and Department of Power			Departmental Enterprises				
Sikkim Power Dev. Corp.	6		1				7

Source: See Annexure 1.10.

The interface problem as well as the absence of a comprehensive frame-work for performance evaluation has affected the functioning of the SLPEs adversely. An appropriate measure of reform should be introduced to remedy this problem. *The initiation of the Memorandum of Understanding (MoU) system is suggested to strengthen the government—SLPEs interface and institute a comprehensive performance evaluation framework.*

The restructuring of the SLPEs would require internal reforms paving the way for OPTIMA. This would require resources for extending voluntary retirement for surplus personnel, instituting management systems (eg., costing, budgeting, pricing, auditing, MIS, manpower planning and recruitment, training and management development, and performance evaluation). The renovation of old and outdated machinery is a must. The computerisation and network support is also required in this context. The enterprises that have been identified in this category comprise SIDICO, State Bank of Sikkim, Sikkim State Co-operative Bank, Sikkim Tourism, Khadi and Village Industries Board, Sikkim National Transport and State Energy and Department of Power and Tea Board of Sikkim. *It is suggested that the GoS may provide a one-time restructuring grant to the enterprises which would continue to be in the state portfolio in the medium term (to be divested at appropriate time after readying them for the purpose) or to be retained in the long run. This grant could be disbursed over a period of three years in a ratio of 34:33:33 depending on the urgency, absorption capacity of the enterprise and the availability of the resources with the government.*

The form of organization plays a significant role in the efficient conduct of a business enterprise. Generally, the government company or the public corporation form is preferred to set up and run the state enterprises. On the contrary, the GoS manages its transport and power sector enterprises in the departmental form. This has affected the performance of these enterprises adversely and deprived them of the enterprise culture. The enterprises in the departmental form do not benefit from the principles of financial management and are not able to interface well with market. As a result, both the transport and power sector enterprises have become a serious drag on the GoS in terms of both the losses making and substantial investments. The departmental enterprises have not shown any will to grow and are found lacking on innovativeness. Although Sikkim is different from many other states in terms of topography, the working of the power sector and transport sector enterprises has been found wanting as compared to their counterparts in the other states of the north-east. It is worth mentioning here that instead of putting in place proper mechanisms to correct this situation, the GoS has taken over the control of some government companies only to vest such control in some government departments. The case of Government Fruit Preservation Factory, Tea Board of Sikkim, Sikkim Poultry Dev. Corp. Ltd, and Sikkim Hatchery Ltd could be cited in this context. *It is suggested that the government may corporatise the departmental enterprises (viz., Sikkim Nationalized Transport and Sikkim Energy and Department of Power) as early as possible and also establish regulatory authorities for their smooth functioning.*

As regards the modalities of privatisation/restructuring, the macro approach has been discussed at length in section 5.2.1. Whereas enterprises found low on all the three dimensions viz., public purpose, profitability and resource mobilization, have to be privatised/wound up through trade sale, employee and management buy out (EMBO), and majority share ownership transfer, the enterprises to be retained need to go in for cold privatisation, OPTIMA, and partial privatisation through joint venture, minority transfer of share ownership, or strategic partnership. In each case an appropriate decision need to be taken by the government. *It is suggested that the government may set up a restructuring board which may deal with such cases from time to time. The Maharashtra Government, Karnataka Government, Punjab Government and the Government of Andhra Pradesh have set up a similar board either through a separate act or executive machinery under the charge of the Department of Finance. The Director (SLPEs) could act as the nodal officer for such machinery.*

Restructuring has to have a human face. This is in line with the present policy on PEs of the UPA government. Both in the cases of closure/privatisation and retention of the SLPEs, the employment in the SLPEs gets affected. These points to the need of social safety net in the SLPEs. The social safety net has five elements: survey of surplus manpower, voluntary retirement, counselling, re-training and re-deployment. The discussions with the SLPEs have revealed that the manpower planning has not received any attention in these enterprises as a result of which they became 'employment boards' and dumping ground of un-required government personnel. In most of the enterprises, the sanctioned strength is far lower than the existing number of personnel/deputations. About 25-30 per cent employees are in excess of the requirement. This affects the work culture in the SLPEs and also adds to the cost of production making their goods and services uncompetitive. *It is suggested that the GoS may formulate a scheme of social safety net for the SLPEs which may assess not only the surplus manpower but also work out the number of employees who could be offered voluntary retirement and benefit from counseling, retraining and redeployment to the maximum possible extent. The government may bear the entire burden of the social safety net. The Director (SLPEs) may be entrusted with the responsibility of formulating and implementing the social safety net programme (SSNP). A special fund of Rs 10 crore may be created for this purpose and placed with Director (SLPEs) as a part of restructuring programme. The Director (SLPEs) could use this fund for social safety net, training and management development, clearing the arrears of accounts of the SLPEs and conducting internal audit, etc.*

We may now compute the total cost of restructuring and propose the allocation of funds for this purpose over a period of three years to make the whole exercise a part of medium-term fiscal planning. This requires us to estimate the value of assets, on the one hand, and work out the restructuring cost, on the other. Annexure 1.11 contains valuation of the SLPEs. As per the Annexure 1.11 the assets owned by the various SLPEs were of the order of Rs 426.50 crore as on March 31, 2004.

Annexure 1.12 contains the estimates of restructuring costs for the enterprises to be retained, on the one hand, and the enterprises to be privatised/wound up, on the other. The restructuring costs relate to voluntary retirement, training, renovation/expansion, write-offs, installation of IT facilities, settlement of court cases, liquidation of bank overdraft, repayment of loans, settlement of contingent liabilities, advertisement and publicity, operational deficit, government guarantees, payment of dues from the government, and working capital assistance. *As suggested earlier, a one time assistance could be provided by the government to meet out these costs which could be disbursed over a period of 3 years in a ratio of 34:33:33. The revenues from privatisation/restructuring need to be used for social safety net and improvement of performance of the enterprises to be retained.*

As noted earlier, some enterprises have to be privatisated/

wound up. The valuation of these enterprises and their restructuring costs is contained in Annexure 1.11 and Annexure 1.12. The general principle that needs to be followed in the case of such enterprises is that if their restructuring costs exceed valuation, the gap has to be made good by the exchequer. However, if the receipts from the sale of these enterprises/their assets, exceed their restructuring costs, the excess of such funds should be utilized for providing social safety net. An analysis of Annexure 1.11 (Valuation of SLPEs) and Annexure 1.12 (Restructuring Cost of SLPEs) reveals that the enterprises to be privatised/wound up were valued at Rs 74.85 crore as on March 31, 2004 whereas, the restructuring cost amounted to Rs 24.96 crore as on the same date. Even if there is a decline in the market value of the assets to the tune of about 50 per cent in the case of the enterprises proposed to be privatised/wound up, there are no funds needed for this purpose from the GoS or any other external source. Annexure 1.12 estimates the gross restructuring cost at Rs 236.98 crore. Rs 24.96 crore has to be deducted from this towards the restructuring of enterprises to be privatised/ wound up as that is going to be a self liquidating exercise. However, Rs 10 crore has to be added to the funds requirements on restructuring as this sum has to be kept at the disposal of the proposed Director (SLPEs) to carry out macro re-engineering of the SLPEs. In sum, the total funds requirement for the restructuring of the SLPEs would be Rs 222.02 crore (composed of Rs 236.98 crore of gross restructuring cost –Rs 24.96 crore of restructuring cost of enterprise to be privatised/wound up +Rs 10 crore as the macro restructuring fund to be kept at the disposal of the Director-SLPEs). This amount could be disbursed over a period of three years to the tune of Rs 75.49 crore, Rs 73.27 crore, Rs 73.27 crore. The privatisation/winding up of the nine enterprises as indicated in Annexure 1.13 is estimated to have saved Rs 35.69 crore in 2003-04.

5.2.2 Micro Approach for Restructuring

This section presents the approach for micro restructuring of the SLPEs.

Name of the SLPE	:	**Sikkim Industrial Development and Investment Corp. Ltd (SIDICO)**
Date of incorporation	:	March, 1977
Classification	:	Financial Sector
Administrative Dep.	:	Finance Revenue and Expenditure Department, GoS.
No of Employees	:	34
Total Investment	:	Rs 19.66 crore
Accumulated Profit/losses	:	Rs –7.36 crore
Dividends	:	Nil
Restructuring Path	:	Disinvest
Anticipated Benefits	:	Additional resources to the GoS
Valuation	:	Nil
Restructuring Cost	:	Rs 35.75 crore

Enterprise Profile

The authorized share capital of the company is Rs 20 crore of which the paid up capital is Rs 17.04 crore. GoS has contributing Rs 10.67 crore to share capital whereas the Industrial Development Bank of India contributed Rs 6.37 crore. The objectives are to: provide long term loans for setting up cottage, tiny, small and medium industries; provide financial support for expansion, diversification and modernisation; extends financial assistance for Hotel Industry, small Hospitals/Nursing homes; provide seed capital towards participation towards promoter's contribution under the scheme of IDBI/SIDBI; participate in share capital for joint sector projects; disburse Central and State Government incentives; set up and develop industrial areas and industrial estates; and achieve rapid industrial and economic development of the State. The corporation has been appointed as a nodal agency for the preparation of the detailed project report for widening of national highway 31 A and setting up the software technology park at Tadong. The major concerns of the corporation include: lack of good and viable proposals for finance, high percentage of NPAs, high administrative cost, decline in equity support from Government, discontinuation of disbursement of central subsidies like central investment subsidies and central transport subsidies, and competition from other financial institutions like commercial banks, North Easter Developmental Financial Institution, SABCCO, etc.

Remarks

Various policy measures taken by the Central Government reforming financial sector and industrial sector have led to the total transformation of the finance industry in India. A healthy competition has stilled the financial sector and the borrower has the choice to go in for a particular lender. There is a need to redefine the role of SIDICO especially in the context of competition being offered by the sister SLPEs such as SABCCO and regional developmental banks such as North Eastern Development Financial Institution. The corporation has high NPAs and also a number of court cases.

Restructuring Costs

	Resources	*Amt. in crore*
1.	Voluntary Retirement Scheme to downsize 25 per cent of manpower	0.90
2.	Training for skill upgradation of staff and for meeting the growing need of business	0.09
3.	Office modernisation, computerisation of financial loan accounting and MIS system	00.10
4.	Industrial Infrastructure and development of Industrial Development center	20.00
5.	Write off (provision made against bad/loss assets as per RBI guideline	12.06
6.	Write off (Provision made for diminution in value of investment as per RBI guidelines)	01.78
7.	Promotional activities viz. Trade fair, publicity, advertisement, entrepreneur development programmes	00.30
8.	Repayment of refinance loan borrowed at higher rate of Interest of 11 per cent	00.37
9.	Dues from Govt. (2 per cent mortgage deed registration Stamp duty incurred by SIDICO as an incentive of entrepreneurs on behalf of State Govt.)	00.09
10.	Fee for conducting a study on financial restructuring	00.06
	Total fund requirement	35.75

Suggested Restructuring

The developmental role of the SIDICO has to be balanced with commercial role. The SIDICO should strike a balance between the investment and lending function and their again between long-term and short-term investments, and long-term and short-term lending's. The corporation requires capital restructuring to access low cost funds in the market to capitalize on its strengths. SIDICO has to strengthen its industry related systems for better credit appraisal. It is advised to convert a part of its equity, say a minimum of Rs 5 crore, into eight per cent long term loan as a first step in the reconstruction of the corporation. The board has to be professionalised in order to tap capital markets. To start with, the GoS may disinvest up to 15 per cent and 20 per cent of its share capital to central financial institutions/mutual funds by fixing bid price through auctions.

Action Plan

- Preparation of a Corporate plan.
- An MOU with Chief Executive to cover aspects such as future role of SIDICO (mix of its lending-investment in shares, term loans, future profits, projected dividends).
- Conversion of equity of Rs 5 crore into 8 per cent term loan.
- VRS to 15 employees, renovations, write off.
- Installation of computer network, hardware and software.
- Advertising and publicity.
- Strengthening industry-wise information databases.
- Designing suitable entrepreneurship training programmes.
- Subjecting all the employees to innovate training programmes in order to regularly update their skills and knowledge base.

Time frame

The total restructuring should be completed within 3 years

Name of the SLPE	:	**State Bank of Sikkim**
Date of incorporation	:	24th June 1968
Classification	:	Financial Sector
Administrative Dep.	:	Finance Revenue and Expenditure Department, GoS.
No of Employees	:	271
Total Investment	:	Rs 5.40 crore
Accumulated Profit/losses	:	Rs 36.42 crore
Dividends	:	–
Restructuring Path	:	Divest
Anticipated Benefits	:	Additional resource to Govt.
Valuation	:	Rs 216.12 crore
Restructuring Cost	:	Rs 37.35

Enterprise Profile

State Bank of Sikkim was founded under the Proclamation of Chogyal. It is a statutory body. The field of operation of the bank is currently restricted to political boundaries of the State of Sikkim. The GoS is the largest client of the bank. The bank also doubles up as the treasury to the State. Among the borrowers, government, contractors, and employees constitute the largest group. There are individual borrowers with large amount of loans and advances. The authorized capital of the bank is Rs 1 crore against the paid up capital of Rs 0.58 crore. The bank has 21 branches all over Sikkim. Although the bank is currently an operational profit making organization, it has accumulated losses of very high magnitude. The bank staff is not well versed in banking operations and is required to acquire relevant skills-set. The Non-Performing Assets (NPAs) of the bank are Rs 40 crore. The bank is looking forward to have a strategic partner for its future growth. The major concerns of the bank are: threat posed by commercial banks, high administrative cost, poor customer services, poor recoveries and inadequate system of monitoring and evaluation.

Remarks

The financial sector reforms are in full swing impacting tremendously the commercial banks. The banks have to fall in line with the capital adequacy, income recognition, NPA reduction, employee professionalisation and technology up-gradation norms. Although the RBI does not regulate State Bank of Sikkim, there is an urgent need for the GoS to extend the linkage of the bank with the Reserve Bank of India (RBI) regulation. The Bank needs to improve its competitiveness and outreach just as the J&K Bank Ltd belonging to the State of Jammu and Kashmir has been doing for itself.

Valuation Details

(Rs. in crore)

Land & Building	*Plant and Machinery*	*Stocks*	*Bank OD*	*Cash*	*Su. Debtors*	*Total*
10.02	–	–	–	185.00	21.10	216.12

Restructuring Cost

(Rs. in crore)

VR	*Writeoff*	*Rennovations*	*Contingent liability*	*Operational deficit*	*Gurantee*	*Write off*	*Total*
5.6	25.24		2.4		4.37		37.35

Suggested Restructuring

The asset-liability mismatch has to be removed. Technological up-gradation leading to setting up of its own network and its interconnection with other networks has to be undertaken. Accumulated losses have to be written-off. Employee training has to be introduced with a great rigour. Court cases have to be settled. Dependence on the GoS has to be considerably reduced for an organic growth of the bank. Loan evaluation procedures have to be tightened.

Action Plan

- Preparation of a corporate plan.
- Application of Indian Banking Companies Act.
- Grant of special fund by government to take care of the losses incurred on account of the loan waiver scheme.
- Settlement of court cases by especially designed institutional mechanism.

- Rigorous training and management development.
- Introduction of loan evaluation procedures.
- VR to excess staff and access to social safety net.

Time Frame

The total restructuring should be completed within 3 years:

Name of the SLPE	: **Sikkim State Co-operative Bank Ltd (SISCO)**
Date of incorporation	: 12th December, 1998
Classification	: Financial Sector
Administrative Dep.	: Department of Co-operation, GoS.
No. of Employees	: 16
Total Investment	: Rs 9.36 crore
Accumulated Profit/Loss	: Rs 1.05 crore
Dividends	: 0.03
Restructuring Path	: Continue in the state sector with increased accent on resource mobilization and profitability
Anticipated Benefits	: Improved fulfillment of public purpose
Valuation	: –
Restructuring Cost	: –

Enterprise Profile

SISCO became the Apex Co-operative Bank after obtaining licence from the Reserve Bank of India. It was registered under the Sikkim Co-operative Societies Act, 1978. The main objectives of SISCO are to: serve as a financing center for all co-operatives societies in the State, raise deposits and share capital for providing loans to member co-operative societies and other individual members against viable schemes, and to do all types of banking business as defined in Section 5 & 6(1) of the Banking Regulation Act, 1949. The authorized capital of the bank is Rs 15 crore. The bank is involved in deposits, and loans and advances operations. It has 3 branches located at Gangtok, Namchi and Gayzing. The bank has been continuously earning profits and also declaring dividends. The credit-deposit (C-D) ratio of the bank is 71 per cent as against the State average of 29 per cent for all the commercial banks. The bank is involved in developing a pilot project in association with the state government, NABARD and 10 co-operative credit societies.

Remarks

The financial sector reforms have added a number of new dimensions for the successful functioning of the banking industry. The co-operative banking sector has emerged as a weak link in the chain. Although, SISCO has been doing well, it has tremendous scope to improve its efficiency. The bank has to improve the volume of its operations and also its outreach. It may also add new businesses and strategise the growth of high value products.

Suggested Restructuring

It is required to concentrate on new product line such as micro finance. It should internalize the use of technology in its operations. It should set-up more number of branches. The bank should promote management development and training. It may consider appointing a consultant to formulate a business growth plan.

Action Plan

- Preparation of a corporate plan
- Networking micro finance institutions
- Setting up more branches
- Technological Upgradation
- Intensive training and management development
- Intra-corporate planning with State Bank of Sikkim

Time frame

The total restructuring should be completed within six months:

Name of the SLPE	:	**Sikkim Jewels Ltd (SJL)**
Date of incorporation	:	7th December, 1972
Classification	:	Manufacturing Sector
Administrative Dep.	:	Department of Commerce and Industries, GoS.

No. of Employees	: 125
Total Investment	: Rs 7.04 crore
Accumulated Profit/Loss	: Rs 0.28 crore
Dividends	: Nil
Restructuring Path	: Closure or Liquidation or total divestiture
Anticipated Benefits	: Saving of Govt. Resources
Valuation	: Rs 2.67 crore
Restructuring Cost	: Rs 21.26 crore

Enterprise Profile

The company is engaged in manufacturing watches, industrial jewels, rotor magnets, and disposable syringes. It provides employment opportunities to unskilled people. The company declared dividends between 1978-79 and 1981-82. However, currently, it is incurring losses due to un-precedented recession in the horological industry. The company has made efforts to overcome the recession by making a dent in the export market. The company has some pending issues for settlement with the government such as the receiving the export incentives, lifting the moratorium on the payment of its deposits and reimbursement of the VRS expenses incurred. The company can take up the manufacturing of any type of micro precession instruments as its manpower trained to produce tiny jewels in micron tolerance.

Remarks

The company has done extremely well in the initial years. A continious decline of domestic demand and fresh investments in new projects without scientific application of project management and evaluation techniques has put company in a tight corner.

Valuation

(*Rs in crore*)

Land & Building	*Plan & Machinery*	*Stocks*	*Sundry Debtors*	*Others*	*Gross Estimated Receipt Total*	*Bank Over-draft*	*Sundry creditors*	*Total*
0.27	0.5	1.52	0.65		2.94		0.27	2.67

Restructuring Cost: Since the enterprise is proposed to be privatised/wound up, the restructuring costs as worked out by us are as follows:

The enterprise revealed the following as the restructuring costs on the presumption that it will continue to be in the state portfolio after restructuring.

Modernisation

1. SJL has a installed capacity of 36 lakhs meter jewels per year and is supplying to domestic markets. As the consumption of water is growing, many state governments are introducing water maters in house holds. This has increased the demand for quality water meters using jewels. SJL proposes to modernize its exiting jewels plants by inducting latest machines form Switzerland and wants to induct high productive diamond wheels. This needs and additional investment of 30 lakhs.
2. SJL is regularly supplying high quality jewels, used in watches, to Switzerland from since five years. Swiss customers are insisting of better quality management. To meet international quality standard, SJL needs modern testing equipments, like profile projectors and higher power microscopes. This needs and additional investment of Rs 40 lakhs.
3. To cut down the rejection and increase productivity of Watch Jewels, SJL wants additional Rs 30 lakhs for importing the latest jewels manufacturing machines from Switzerland.

Diversification

1. *Disposable syringe and needle manufacturing unit*: SJL has set-up a pilot project to manufacturing Disposable syringes with a capacity of one millions syringes per year. Commercial production is expected to commence from 3rd week of April 2005. SJL plans to increase the capacity to 10 millions per year by inducting latest machines from Austria at a cost of Rs 250 lakhs.
2. *Rotor magnets for quartz watches*: SJL is manufacturing Rotor Magnets from rare earth material, Samarium Cobalt, and

has supplied to watch manufacturers in India. To export this product abroad, as the clients wants complete stepper motor, SJL wants an additional investment of Rs 700 lakhs to induct latest technology ie., sintering machine from Singapore. Detail project report can be submitted.

3. *Technical Training and Traveling*: To be more competitive in international market SJL wants to improve the technical skills of manpower by training them in Europe. To develop new markets internationally, marketing persons have to travel frequently and freely. This needs additional fund of Rs 50 lakhs.
4. *Computerisation and Research and Development*: To be more efficient computerisation and interlinking of various departments to share information and data is must. Also to be more efficient Research and Development activity should be taken up seriously for technology upgradation to look for various options for diversification using similar technology. An additional fund of Rs 50 lakhs is needed for the same.
5. *Voluntary Retirement Scheme*: To cut down the cost of production and to be more scheme and a fund of Rs 49.32 lakhs was provided for the same.
6. *Salary Revision*: Salary of the employees was last revised in the year 1998 and needs revision now which will need and additional fund of Rs 20 lakhs
7. *Sundry Payable*: Rs 27.03 lakhs
8. *Contingent liabilities*: SJL has given guarantee for the loan taken by ancillary units; 5 units finance by SIDICO – Rs 169 lakhs, 5 units financed by IDBI –Rs 276 lakhs

Suggested Restructuring

The organization is a clear case for privatisation. As an alternative, the organization could be merged in a holding company and made one of its division. The holding company, in due course, decide about the continuation of the division or its privatisation/closure.

Action Plan

- Valuation of assets and liabilities
- VR to excess employees

- Access to social safety net
- Training and management development on war footing in case of continuation of the company
- Merger related activities if the company has to be made a division of the proposed holding company

Time Frame

The total restructuring should be completed in six months.

Name of the SLPE	: **Sikkim Poultry Development Corp. Ltd**
Date of incorporation	: March 1991
Category	: Manufacturing Sector
Administrative Dep.	: Animal Husbandry LF&VS Department
No. of Employees	: 6
Total Investment	: Rs 0.79 crore
Accumulated losses	: –
Dividends	: Nil
Restructuring Path	: Closure or Liquidation or total divestiture
Anticipated Benefits	: Saving of Govt. Resources
Valuation	: Rs 0.70 crore
Restructuring Cost	: Rs 1.95 crore

Enterprise Profile

The corporation was established to promote, administer, own and run, improve, develop, finance directly or indirectly, store and sale poultry and poultry products, poultry feed and equipment, and provide services for the growth of poultry industry. The activities of the corporation include financial promotion and welfare of the public and the poultry farmers, trading of the inputs, selling poultry and poultry products and operating poultry processing plant and egg power processing plant. The enterprises functions in competitive market. The finances of the enterprise are in a very unhealthy shape. Besides negative net profits, the same trend persists with regard to net worth and working capital. The corporation is seeking a turnaround based on a project report prepared by a consultant.

Remarks

The organization is defunct and is not adding any value to any stakeholder.

Valuation	Amt Rs in crore
Land and Building	0.70 crore
Plant and Machinery	Nil
Bank Overdraft	Nil
Patients	Nil
Su. Debtors	Nil
Others	Nil
Total	0.70 crore

Restructuring Cost	Rs in crore
VRS	Nil
Training	0.15
Renovation and Expansion	1.50
Writeoff	Nil
IT requirement	Nil
Court Cases	Nil
Bank OD	Nil
Repayment of Loans	Nil
Contingent liabilities	0.10
Operational Deficit	0.10
Advertisement and promotion	0.10
Su. Creditors	Nil
Guarantees	Nil
Others	Nil
Dues from Government	Nil
Total	1.95

Suggested Restructuring

The organization could be privatised through trade sale/employee and management buy out (EMBO)/joint venture

Action Plan

- Valuation of assets and liabilities.
- VR to excess employees.

- Access to social safety net.
- Training and management development on war footing in case of continuation of the company.
- Merger related activities if the company has to be made a division of the proposed holding company.

Time Frame

The total restructuring should be completed in six months.

Name of the SLPE	: **Sikkim Hatchery Ltd**
Date of incorporation	: August 1994
Category	: Manufacturing Sector
Administrative Dep.	: Animal Husbandry LF&VS Department
No. of Employees	: 15
Total Investment	: Rs 0.46 crore
Accumulated Profit/Loss	: –
Dividends	: Nil
Restructuring Path	: Closure or Liquidation or total divestiture
Anticipated Benefits	: Saving of Govt. Resources
Valuation	: Rs 2.50 crore
Restructuring Cost	: Rs 5.20 crore

Enterprise Profile

Sikkim Hatchery Ltd was set-up as a joint sector company by GoS and Sri Venkateswara Hatcheries Ltd.—a private sector company. The organization was established to satisfy the demand for hatchery products within the Sikkim and Bhutan. The company maintains poultry breeder stock, produces commercial chicks, markets chicks to the poultry farmer, runs a feed mill and supplies brooding equipment to the poultry farms. The company produces day old broiler chicks. The company is in manufacturing sector and operates in competitive market. The company operates at 25 per cent of its capacity.

Remarks

The organization is defunct and is not adding any value to any stakeholder.

Suggested Restructuring

The organization could be privatised through trade sale/employee and management buy out (EMBO)/joint venture

Action Plan

- Valuation of assets and liabilities
- VR to excess employees
- Access to social safety net
- Training and management development on war footing in case of continuation of the company
- Merger related activities if the company has to be made a division of the proposed holding company

Time Frame

The total restructuring should be completed in six months.

Name of the SLPE	:	**Sikkim Precision Industries Ltd (SPIL)**
Date of incorporation	:	15th February 1999
Classification	:	Manufacturing Sector
Administrative Dep.	:	Department of Commerce and Industries, GoS.
No. of Employees	:	60
Total Investment	:	Rs 3.70 crore
Accumulated Profit/Loss	:	Rs –0.02 crore
Dividends	:	Nil
Restructuring Path	:	Closure or Liquidation or total divestiture
Anticipated Benefits	:	Saving of Govt. Resources
Valuation	:	Rs 7.62 crore
Restructuring Cost	:	Rs 4.00 crore

Enterprise Profile

The company is involved in manufacturing operations and produces T0-92 and T0-220 semi conductors. For its order book, it is completely dependent on Bharat Electronics Ltd (BEL) which places job order on the company and supplies relevant inputs. The company provides employment to 50 persons with primary and secondary school education background. The company faces fierce competition from China which supplies the semi conductors at much lower prices. The company is looking for new markets. It is approaching Bharat Heavy Electrical's Ltd (BHEL) to supply capacitors, and replace some of its old machinery. The company is planning to acquire some new machinery to boost its production. It is operating at a capacity of 40 per cent.

Remarks

SPIL is a high end technology oriented company operating in a completely protective environment. The support from its mother organization—BEL, is not coming forward in as much as it is required. It is facing threat from China. It has excess manpower. Its capacity utilisation is very low.

Suggested Restructuring

As per the company executives, SPIL should restructure its product line, markets and technology. The excess manpower could be offered VR. The company may setup T0 – 92 assembly plant within the same premises. The company may also take steps to increase its capacity utilisaiton.

However, in our opinion, the organization could be privatised through trade sale/employee and management buy out (EMBO)/ joint venture

Action Plan

- Valuation of assets and liabilities
- VR to excess employees
- Access to social safety net
- Training and management development on war footing in case of continuation of the company
- Merger related activities if the company has to be made a division of the proposed holding company

Time Frame

The total restructuring should be completed in six months.

Name of the SLPE	:	**Sikkim Time Corporation Ltd (SITCO)**
Date of incorporation	:	1976
Classification	:	Manufacturing Sector
Administrative Dep.	:	Department of Industries, GoS.
No. of Employees	:	146
Total Investment	:	Rs 11.74 crore
Accumulated Profit/Loss	:	Rs –2.92 crore
Dividends	:	Nil
Restructuring Path	:	Closure or Liquidation or total divestiture
Anticipated Benefits	:	Saving of Govt. Resources
Valuation	:	Rs 2.69 crore
Restructuring Cost	:	Rs 23.21 crore

Enterprise Profile

The company is the only watch manufacturer unit in Sikkim. It is the first company in Sikkim to have a country-wide marketing network. The company started mechanical watch assembly unit in technical collaboration with HMT Ltd. It established a watch crown manufacturing unit in collaboration with HMT Ltd in 1984. In 1987, the company set up a semi-conductor unit in collaboration with Bharat Electronics Ltd. In 1992, the company established a digital watch manufacturing unit in collaboration with HMT Ltd. In 2001, the company established a TV speaker manufacturing unit in collaboration with BPL Ltd. The collaborations have run into rough weather due to problems with the mother units. The company has provided employment to over 1000 people mostly school dropouts from poor and rural backgrounds. Ninty per cent of the employees of the company are women folk. The company has contributed towards integration of Sikkim with the rest of the country by promoting business association, transfer of technology and collaborations with enterprises of repute such as the HMT Ltd, Bharat Electronics Ltd and BPL Ltd. The company fosters industrial culture in the State. Presently, the undertaking operates at a capacity of 20-30 per cent.

Remarks

The company's order book is empty. It has a huge campus which is not being put to any proper use. The employees sit idle without work. There is no money with the company to buy raw materials and pay wages.

Valuation

(*Rs in crore*)

Land & Building	*Plant & Machinery*	*Stocks*	*Sundry Debtors*	*Others*	*Bank Over-draft*	*Sundry creditors*	*7+8*	*Valuation*
1	2	3	4	5	6	7		
0.71	14.29	4.57	2.59	0.07	5.77	0.4	6.17	23.15

Restructuring Cost	**Amt Rs in crore**
VRS	2.19
Training	0.35
Renovation and expansion	2.85
Writeoffs	1.50
IT requirement	0.30
Court cases	Nil
Bank overdrafts	5.78
Contingent liabilities	Nil
Operational Deficit	2.54
Advertisement and sales promotion	1.80
Su. Creditors	0.40
Repayment	0.51
Gurantees	5.00
Total	23.21

Suggested Restructuring

The organization could be privatised through trade sale/employee and management buy out (EMBO)/joint venture

Action Plan

- Valuation of assets and liabilities
- VR to excess employees

- Access to social safety net
- Training and management development on war footing in case of continuation of the company

Time Frame

The total restructuring should be completed in six months.

Name of the SLPE	:	**Tea Board of Sikkim**
Date of incorporation	:	1st June 1974
Classification	:	Manufacturing Sector
Administrative Dep.	:	Department of Commerce and Industries, GoS
No. of Employees	:	449
Total Investment	:	Rs 22.71 crore
Accumulated Profit/loss	:	Rs 7.83 crore
Dividends	:	Nil
Restructuring Path	:	Continue in the state sector with increased accent on resource mobilisation and profitability
Anticipated Benefits	:	Improved fulfillment of public purpose
Valuation	:	Rs 4.35 crore
Restructuring Cost	:	Rs 0.72crore

Enterprise Profile

It is a manufacturing enterprise presently being controlled by the Department of Industries and Commerce. Tea Board of Sikkim produces tea from the Temi Tea gardens spread over in an area of 350 acres. It is a profitable enterprise. However, due to global recession, its profits are declining. It provides employment to a large number of local people. It has been able to build a brand for itself. The plant and machinery of the corporation is becoming obsolete and outdated. Although, there is a board to manage the organisation, the commercial outlook does not find favour with the organization place because of excessive control of the administrative department. In the recent years, the production and productivity of the board had been declining.

Remarks

Tea board continues to remain unprofessional. Its bushes are becoming old. It has not been able to increase area of tea plantation. Its tea leaf withering plant and tea leaf drier machines are growing obsolete. Although, it had a brand known as Temi Tea, it has not been able to popularize its tea on par with Darjiling Tea. The wage costs of the company are increasing due to a substantial revision in the minimum wages.

Valuation

(Rs in crore)

Land & Building	*Plan & Machinery*	*Stocks*	*Sundry Debtors*	*Others*	*Cash Bank balance and investments*	*Total*
4.35	–	–	–	–	–	4.35

Restructuring Cost

(Rs in crore)

VR	*Training*	*Renovation/Expansion*	*Writeoff*	*Total*
–	–	0.70	–	0.70

Suggested Restructuring

The board should be converted into a co-operative society which may obtain the near by lands for the tea plantations. Old plants and machines should be replaced. The newly formed co-operative society may even examine the option of taking the near by plots on lease. The productivity growth is the need of the hour. Alternatively, the board could be merged in the newly proposed holding company for the manufacturing sector and run as one of its division.

Action Plan

- Preparation of a corporate plan
- Conversion into a co-operative society or inclusion as a division of the holding company for manufacturing sector.

- Valuation of assets and liabilities
- Professional marketing
- Replacement of old plant and machinery.
- OPTIMA
- Acquisition of nearby plots

Time Frame

The total restructuring should be completed in six months.

Name of the SLPE	: **Government Fruit Preservation Factory (GFPF)**
Date of incorporation	: 1964-65
Classification	: Manufacturing Sector
Administrative Dep.	: Department of Industries and Commerce
No. of Employees	: 63
Total Investment	: Rs 1.07 crore
Accumulated Profit/loss	: Rs 0.60 crore
Dividends	: Nil
Restructuring Path	: Introduce financial adjustments and then go for disinvestment
Anticipated Benefits	: Long term Investment in service to consumers
Valuation	: Rs 3.12 crore
Restructuring Cost	: Rs 1.78 crore

Enterprise Profile

Government Fruit Preservation Factory (GFPF) undertakes the processing of fruits to produce fruit juices, jams, jellies and sauces. Initially, the factory was producing only orange squash in season to encourage farmers to grow orange plantation. Later on manufacturing of Jam, Jelly of other fruits like Pineapple, Plum Mango, were also introduced, while establishing the factory. The Maharaja had an understanding with Government of India to supply produce of the factory to the establishments of the Defence Ministry, Government of India. The products were later supplied to Indian Airline, Air India, and British Airways, etc. These channels of marketing continued to remain in vogue after the merger of Sikkim into India. The company was marketing its products under the brand '*Sikkim Supreme*'. The firm was privatised and handed over to M/s Sikkim Food and General Industries (P) Ltd. in 1987—a firm owned by a local businessman. The firm could not manage in the business world which adversely effected the goodwill of Sikkim Supreme Brand. The firm was black listed by the Defence Department and subsequently handed over to the state government. The factory remained closed for one year. 1995, the GoS handed over the factory to a Swiss firm M/s Red Orchid Food Processing Ltd to run the company as a joint venture. However, the Swiss firm deserted the company and consequently the GoS has to takeover the firm again. Now, GFPF is managed by the Department of Industries and Commerce. Although, the firm is earning profits it faces a tough competition from private sector. Its counter parts in Bhutan holds a major sway in the markets and is able to sell its goods under the '*Druk Brand*'. Kissan, another Indian firm, is also a formidable competitor. Many small firms producing fruit juices, jelly's, and sauces in West Bengal have reduced the market share of the GFPF. The moderinisation proposal granted by the Ministry of Food Processing, GoI, has not received support from the GoS. The capacity utilized is very low and is in the range of 10-20 per cent.

Remarks

The government is not sure about the future of the factory as it faces tremendous competition from private sector especially from Kissan and Bhutan's Druk. The Factory's brand image has lost sheen. The Factory's fortune has been fluctuating. This makes the company a very good case for total privatisation.

Valuation

(*Rs in crore*)

Land & Building	*Plan & Machinery*	*Stocks*	*Sundry Debtors*	*Others*	*Total*
1	1.5	0.5	0.12	–	3.12

Restructuring Cost

A. Machinery and Equipments	Rs. in crore
1. Automatic bottom machine 24-30 BPM EVATS	0.05
2. Pet blowing machine SSB05B (upto 2 Lts)	0.05
3. Water processing system 2000 LPM RO	0.05
4. SS Tank and Pipe lines	0.01
5. Packing set: Stripper, labeling machine (injection moulding)	0.08
6. Homogenous machine SS conveyer etc.	0.03
7. Bottle washing machine	0.01
8. M .... Crane of one ton	0.01
9. Shreading machine	0.05
10. Boiler 600 kg	0.05
11. Pouch packing machine	0.02
12. Electric lifting platform (4 pes × 1.3 lakhs)	0.02
13. Retort (2 Nos.)	0.02
14. SS Kettle (4 pec × 1.00 each)	0.02
15. Smoke exhust system	0.02
16. Transport 709 model TATA truck	0.08
17. Office Vehicle	0.05
18. Food grade containers 1000 nos @ 300 pes	0.03
	0.69
Installation Cost 5 per cent	0.03
	0.72
Transportation 5 per cent	0.03
	0.75

B. Civil Construction Works	Amt. in Lakhs
1. Replacement of wooden trust by sheet tins inproduction hall	0.04
2. Flooring of production hall with Kota stone 150 × 30 & 50 × 50 @ 80 sq ft	0.06
3. Tiles upto 7 sft height in production hall	0.03
4. Renovation drainage system	0.02
5. Painting of factory roof and wall approach road	0.01
6. Office building repairing	0.01
7. Constuction of RCC 2 tier platform for stocking pupl (Raw Material) in carboys	0.02
8. Renovation of electrification	0.03

9. Renovation of steam line	0.01
	0.24
C. Extension Working—Marketing Expenses	**0.15**

In metropolitans cities like Kolkata, New Delhi, Jaipur etc.

Restructuring Cost

VR	*Plant & Machinery*	*Training*	*Renovation/ Expansion*	*Advertisement & Promotional*	*Guarantees*	*Total*
0.63	–	–	0.99	0.15	–	1.78

Suggested Restructuring

The company could be privatised through trade sale or as a minority joint venture.

Action Plan

- Valuation of assets and liabilities
- VR to excess employees
- Access to social safety net
- Appointment of merchant banker for privatisation

Time Frame

The total restructuring should be completed in six months.

Name of the SLPE	: **Sikkim Co-operative Milk Producers Union Ltd**
Date of incorporation	: July 1980
Classification	: Manufacturing Sector
Administrative Dep.	: Co-operation Department, GoS
No. of Employees	: 83
Total Investment	: Rs 0.14 crore
Accumulated Profit/loss	: Rs –2.54 crore
Dividends	: Nil
Restructuring Path	: Disinvest
Anticipated Benefits	: Additional resource to Govt.
Valuation	: Rs 0.98 crore
Restructuring Cost	: Rs 3.37 crore

Enterprise Profile

It is an Apex body of the primary milk producers' co-operative societies at the village level and is a replica of AMUL. It is a manufacturing enterprise hamstrung with the following problems: low productivity of cows due to poor genetic potential, inadequacy of support services, inadequacy of fund, high cost of milk procurement and marketing, lack of feeds and fodder resources, weak extension services, high cost of maintenance of old plant and machinery, high establishment cost due to excess manpower, and weak resources and infrastructure for quality control. The organization utilizes 70 per cent of its capacity. The organization has ambitious plans for restructuring of diverse types and also meeting the challenges emerging from competition. Currently, the enterprise is incurring losses and its net worth is receding.

Remarks

Sikkim Milk Union is engaged in the task of rural development through livestock growth and dairy sector promotion. It faces competition from Anand and also from organized dairies and unorganized milk producers. The organisation may make more milk producer's societies as its members and pay-off partly the shareholdings of the GoS.

Valuation

(Rs in crore)

Land & Building	*Plan & Machinery*	*Stocks*	*Sundry Debtors*	*Others*	*Total*
0.05	0.8	0.13			0.98

Restructuring Cost

(Rs in crore)

VR	*Training*	*Renovation/ Expansion*	*Write off*	*IT requirement*	*Court cases*	*Bank overdraft*	*Repayment of loans*	*Contingent labilities*	*Operational deficit*	*Total*
1.13		0.11		0.17			0.05	0.30	1.61	3.37

Suggested Restructuring: Sikkim Milk Producers Union requires to undertake market restructuring, financial restructuring, manpower restructuring and technological restructuring. It also requires to initiate a cost restructuring drive. The market restructuring requires contracting out of milk distribution, setting up milk parlors in Gangtok, producing more value added items and better packaging. Manpower restructuring requires VR to excess work force, capacity building and appointment of qualified manpower. Technological restructuring requires installation of electric bulk milk coolers, automation of milk testing procedures, and computerisation cost control requires the setting up of standards and their vigorous implementation.

Action Plan

- Asset-liability valuation
- VR to excess employees
- Joint ventures for marketing the products
- Technological upgradation
- Outsourcing of milk distribution
- Reduction in milk collection costs

Time Frame

The total restructuring should be completed in six months.

Name of the SLPE	: **Sikkim Tourism Development Corp. Ltd**
Date of incorporation	: 21st September 1998
Classification	: Promotional Sector
Administrative Dep.	: Department of Tourism, GoS
No. of Employees	: 89
Total Investment	: Rs 6.06 crore
Accumulated Profit/loss	: Rs –2.59 crore
Dividends	: Nil
Restructuring Path	: Continue in the state sector with increased accent on resource mobilisation and profitability
Anticipated Benefits	: Improved fulfilment of public purpose

Valuation : Rs 3.52 crore
Restructuring Cost : Rs 8.83 crore

Enterprise Profile

The corporation deals with tourism services which includes tourist accommodation, tourist cafeteria, tourist transport (helicopter service) and marketing, and consultancy to tourism department. The corporation also organizes Teesta Tea Tourism festival. The corporation handles package tours and also conducts management events. The corporation provides leadership to tourism industry in Sikkim in organising capacity building programme and initiating development of tourism to various places in Sikkim. The corporation operates at 50 per cent of the capacity in terms of occupancy rate of its hotels.

Remarks

Sikkim offers a great scope for tourism. The corporation has not been able to come up to the expectations. It can enhance its productivity in relation to providing quality tourist services. It needs to introduce an effective cost management. The *mantra* for the future growth of the corporation should be 'Public-Private-Partnership' (PPP). The GoS should handover the Nortel Hotel to the corporation purely from the point of view of safeguarding its financial viability. The corporation should take steps to improve the occupancy of its hotel accommodation. It should undertake aggressive marketing of its services. It should professionalise its staff. The Department of Tourism, GoS should facilitate in the efficient functioning of the corporation.

Valuation

(Rs in crore)

Land &Building	*Plant & Machinery*	*Stocks*	*Bank overdraft*	*Patents*	*Sundry Debtors*	*Others*	*Total*
3.27	NA	NA	Nil	Nil	0.25	Nil	3.51

Restructuring Costs

(Rs in crore)

VR	*Training*	*Renovation*	*Write off*	*IT requirement*	*Court cases*	*Bank OD*	*Repayment of loans*	*Contingent liability*	*Operational deficit*	*Advertisement*	*Su. Cr*	*Total*
0.33	0.35	2.50	Nil	1.25	Nil	Nil	Nil	1.05	Nil	0.03	2.31	8.83

Suggested Restructuring

The corporation should concentrate on promotion of tourism in Sikkim and reduce its direct involvement in providing services which it could better lease out, divest through trade sale or franchise to private sector.

Action Plan

- Preparation of a corporate plan
- Valuation of assets and liabilities
- Installation of management and financial systems
- Taking over of Nortel hotel
- Concentrating on promotional role
- Leasing out, franchising or divesting directly productive activities
- Development of tourist cites on PPP basis
- Installation of website and ensuring its proper functioning
- Professionalisation of staff
- Management development and training for capacity building
- VR to excess employees
- Access to social safety net

Time Frame

The total restructuring should be completed in six months.

Name of the SLPE	: **Sikkim Handloom and Handicrafts Dev. Corp. Ltd**
Date of incorporation	: 1st December 2003
Classification	: Promotional Sector
Administrative Dep.	: Department of Commerce and Industries, GoS
No. of Employees	: 13
Total Investment	: Rs 0.80 crore
Accumulated Profit/Loss	: Rs 0.05 crore
Dividends	: Nil
Restructuring Path	: Continue in the state sector with increased accent on resource mobilisation and profitability
Anticipated Benefits	: Improved fulfilment of public purpose
Valuation	: Rs 1.23 crore
Restructuring Cost	: Rs 13.70 crore

Enterprise Profile

Sikkim Handloom and Handicrafts Dev. Corp. Ltd started operation effect from December 1, 2003. The corporation has a share capital of Rs 5 crore. It is involved in the promotion of handloom and handicrafts development activities. It organizes training programmes for artisans to upgrade their skills. It also provides marketing support to craft persons, craft societies, co-operatives and non-government organisations. Apart from providing marketing outlets through the sales emporium at Gangtok and Delhi, the corporation also encourages the participation of the craft persons in various exhibitions and fares within the State, as well as, at the national level.

Remarks

The corporation is involved in the vital task of preserving and fostering the handicrafts wealth of Sikkim and enhancing the competencies of artisans. Its effort to promote handicrafts through a pilot project by setting up nine craft co-operatives at various places in the State is appreciable. The corporation's showroom at Gangtok is functioning well. The corporation needs to step up its pace of work, professionalise its management, come out of the shadow of the parent department, step up its effort in the realm of marketing and ensure a longer tenure for the chief executive. The corporation needs revamp its managerial set up. It should promote networking with the private sector institutions.

Valuation

(Rs in crore)

Land & Building	Plan & Machinery	Stocks	Sundry Debtors	Others	Cash Bank balance and investments	Total
0.93	0.22	0.08				1.23

Restructuring Cost

(Rs in crore)

VR	Training	Renovations	Contingent liability	Operational deficit	Advertisement	Total
Nil	0.50	7.00	1.2	5.00	Nil	13.70

Suggested Restructuring

The corporation needs to develop its brand image. The corporation needs to enhance its commercial viability and put premium on entrepreneurship. It should concentrate on developmental/ promotional role. It should open showrooms on franchise basis. It may lease out its existing showroom at zero point at Gangtok. A lease agreement for a period of 3 to 5 years may be negotiated.

Action Plan

- Preparation of Corporate Plan
- Professionalizing management through intensive training in the areas of functional management
- Promoting management systems and their strict adherence
- Enhancing the developmental role and minimizing commercial role
- Brand building

- Extending the sales outlet networks through franchising
- Leasing out the facility at zero point to private sector

Time Frame

The total restructuring should be completed in six months.

Name of the SLPE	: **Khadi and Village Industries Board (KVIB)**
Date of incorporation	: 1975
Category	: Promotional Sector
Administrative Dep.	: Department of Commerce and Industries, GoS
No. of Employees	: 83
Total Investment	: Rs 12.01 crore
Accumulated losses	: –
Dividends	: –
Restructuring Path	: Continue in the state sector with increased accent on resource mobilisation and profitability
Anticipated Benefits	: Improved fulfilment of public purpose
Valuation	: Rs 2.03 crore
Restructuring Cost	: Rs 1.59 crore

Enterprise Profile

Prior to the merger of Sikkim in the Indian Union, the activities of the board were being managed with the help of Bihar Khadi and Village Industries Board. Presently, the board is operating 13 production and service centers, seven sales centers and four departmental units in different districts of Sikkim. The board has been operating one rural engineering works and also a hand made paper industry unit. The board was set up to patronise Khadi and Village industries in the State. The board produces cotton and woolen khadi, and village industries Products. It is a promotional enterprise. It is incurring losses. The establishment costs of the board are very high. The finances of the board are not in a good shape. The productivity is very low and the market push for its products is non-existent.

Remarks

Khadi and Village Industries Board serves a high social purpose. However, its not being run professionally. Its dependence on the government is very high. Its innovative capability is very low. Its establishment costs are exorbitant. Its marketing capabilities are questionable. The functioning of the board has not much helped the spinners and weavers in ameliorating their poverty.

Valuation

(Rs in crore)

Land & Building	Plan & Machinery	Stocks	Sundry Debtors	Others	Total
–	–	–	0.58	1.45	2.03

Restructuring Cost	*Rs in crore*
Payment of retirement benefits on VRS scheme	0.65
Overdraft	0.34
Purchase of new *Charkha* and *Kharga*	0.07
Setting up of a woken milling plant	0.15
Repairs and renewals	0.03
Stipend	0.10
Business development	0.25
Total	1.59

Suggested Restructuring

There is a need to amend the Khadi and Village Industries Board Act de-linking the board from the government. The establishment costs have to be reduced drastically. The managerial capability of the personnel is required to be enhanced through management development and training. The surplus employees need to be covered by VRS. The repairs and renovations should be given top priority for a smooth functioning of the board. The board should aggressively work towards increasing its turnover.

Action Plan

- Preparation of a corporate plan
- VRS to surplus employees
- Access to safety net
- Management development and training on war footing
- Renovation and repairs of plant and machinery
- Installation of financial and management systems
- Sustain increase in turnover
- Focusing on development of village industries products

Time Frame

The total restructuring should be completed in six months.

Name of the SLPE	: **State Trading Corporation (STC)**
Date of incorporation	: 30th March 1972
Classification	: Trading and Service Enterprise
Administrative Dep.	: Department of Commerce and Industries, GoS
No. of Employees	: 108
Total Investment	: Rs 1.11 crore
Accumulated Profit/loss	: –
Dividends	: Rs 0.11 crore
Restructuring Path	: Introduce financial adjustments and then go in for disinvestment
Anticipated Benefits	: Long term Investment in service to consumers
Valuation	: Rs 32.50 crore
Restructuring Cost	: Rs 5.52 crore

Enterprise Profile

The corporation is engaged in procurement and supply of all types of materials required by the GoS. In addition to attending the protocol duties of the GoS, the corporation also renders all types of assistance to the patients sent to Kolkata for medical treatment. The corporation has an equity capital of Rs 1.11 crore. It has no long term debt. It is a profit earning enterprise. The corporation proposes to close down the loss making branches at Kolkata and Siliguri. It runs on a margin of three per cent between the procurement price and the price at which goods are sold to the government departments. The wages and salaries constitute about seven per cent of the total cost incurred by the corporation. The corporation is saddled with excess manpower. It proposes to extend VRS to 25 employees. The corporation faces recovery problems from the government departments. The corporation is awaiting a face lift from the opening up of the Nathulla-Pass linking India to China. The corporation operates in a highly competitive market where private sector enterprises are emerging as more important entities. The government departments are not satisfied with the functioning of the corporation. The corporation, as an intermediate agency between the GoS and suppliers, only adds to the procurement costs and delays.

Remarks

The management and financial systems of the corporation are very weak. The manpower is not trained. The turnover is inadequate. Although, the corporation is a profit making organization, it has not nurtured the climate of innovation. It is facing tough competition from private sector. Its recoveries are not satisfactory. There is a need to privatise the corporation.

Suggested Restructuring

The GoS has to repeal the act which paved the way for the setting up of the corporation. The GoS may privatise the corporation through trade sale/lease/employee and management buyout.

Action Plan

- Updation of accounts
- Repeal of the act under which the enterprise was set up
- VRS to excess employees
- Action plan for recoveries
- Appointment of merchant bankers for privatisation
- Preparation and implementation of action plan for recoveries

Time frame

The total restructuring should be completed in six months.

Name of the SLPE	:	**The Denjong Agricultural Co-operative Society (DACS)**
Date of incorporation	:	8th February 1965
Classification	:	Trading and Service Enterprise
Administrative Dep.	:	Co-operation Department, GoS.
No. of Employees	:	112
Total Investment	:	Rs 0.2 crore
Accumulated Profit/loss	:	Rs –0.83 crore
Dividends	:	–
Restructuring Path	:	Increased accent on the resource mobilisation/partial disinvestment
Anticipated Benefits	:	Better Revenues or reduced budget support
Valuation	:	Rs 0.71 crore
Restructuring Cost	:	Rs 8.40 crore

Enterprise Profile

This Apex co-operative society undertakes marketing of agricultural produce and supplies of consumables to army. It is a trading and service enterprise. The organization is planning for expansion and diversification of its activities. It proposes to initiate business development by setting up flour mill, cold storage, transport fleet, meat procession units, marketing chain outlets and departmental store projects. It is expecting financial support from National Co-operative Development Corporation (NCDC) and North East Council (NEC).

Remarks

The enterprise was set-up to serve the interests of army in the region. It should diversify the business and reduce the dependence on army. It could set up wholesale and retail outlets throughout the State. It is duplicating some of the activities with Sikkim Consumer Co-operative Society, SIMFED, and STC.

Suggested Restructuring

The organisation should undertake marketing, financial, manpower and technological restructuring to curb infructuous expenses, rationalize manpower, develop infrastructural activities, and modernise its associated units. It should be a part of the proposed newly merged organisation integrating into itself SIMFED, STC and Sikkim Consumer Co-operative Society.

Action Plan

- Preparation of a corporate plan
- Valuation of assets
- Assessment of liabilities
- Legal, accounting and financial preparation for merger into the proposed composite entity
- Appointment of a consultant to effect merger

Time frame

The total restructuring should be completed in six months.

Name of the SLPE	: **Sikkim Consumers Co-operative Society**
Date of incorporation	: 23rd July, 1975
Classification	: Trading and Service Enterprise
Administrative Dep.	: Co-operation Department, GoS.
No of Employees	: 27
Total Investment	: Rs 0.17 crore
Accumulated Profit/loss	: Rs 0.75 crore
Dividends	: –
Restructuring Path	: Introduce financial adjustments and then go in for disinvestment
Anticipated Benefits	: Long term Investment in service to consumers
Valuation	: Rs 2.32 crore
Restructuring Cost	: Rs 1.62 crore

Enterprise Profile

The organisation caters to the needs of the general public by providing services at right price and acting as a countervailing force to balance the prices offered by the private sector. It is a consumer co-operative society dealing with the supply of stationeries, crockeries and other sundry items to the departments of the GoS and the central government agencies. It has also some retail counters. Initially, the society was handling consumer goods including the public distribution services items and the distribution of controlled cloths. The society makes purchases of all the commodities directly through the manufacturer and the wholesale agencies. The society proposes to open up departmental stores, install paper cutting units and set up sub-divisional stores.

Remarks

The enterprise is operating in highly competitive market and is involved in non-core activities. Denjong, SIMFED and STC are duplicating its activities. Some other SLPEs are also planning to take up the same activities. Although, the enterprise is profit making, it does not have professional staff. Its accounts are in arrears. It faces an acute problem of working capital. It does not have its own office premises. It is trying to become a wholesale agent for several companies. Its turnover is inadequate. It does not have a strong middle management. Its financial and managemental systems are weak.

Valuation

(Rs in crore)

Land &Building	*Plant & Machinery*	*Stocks*	*Patients*	*Su. Debts*	*Others*	*Total*
0.90	0.20	0.40	–	0.82	–	2.32

Restructuring Cost

(Rs in crore)

VR	*Training*	*Renovation*	*Write off*	*IT required*	*Advertisement*	*Dues from Govt*	*Total*
0.81	0.02	–	0.03	0.12	0.05	0.59	1.62

Suggested Restructuring

The organization should be merged into a broader entity combining SIMFED and Denjong Agricultural Co-operative Society. It should clear the arrears of its accounts.

Action Plan

- The arrears of accounts should be completed as early as possible
- Preparation of a corporate plan
- The VRS could be offered to surplus employees
- The merger proceedings should be initiated
- The liabilities should be settled and receivables may be obtained
- Legal, accounting and financial preparation for merger into the proposed composite entity
- Appointment of a consultant to effect merger

Time Frame

The total restructuring should be completed in 1 year.

Name of the SLPE	:	**Sikkim State Co-operative Supply and Marketing Federation Ltd (SIMFED)**
Date of incorporation	:	1983
Classification	:	Trade and Service
Administrative Dep.	:	Co-operation Department, GoS.
No of Employees	:	40
Total Investment	:	Rs 1.02 crore
Accumulated losses	:	–
Dividends	:	–
Restructuring Path	:	Increased accent on the resource mobilisation/partial disinvestment.
Anticipated Benefits	:	Better Revenues or reduced budget support
Restructuring Cost	:	Rs 29.65 crore

Enterprise Profile

The authorized capital of the Federation is Rs 3 crore. This organisation is involved in the marketing of agricultural produce viz. ginger, orange, cardamom. The organisation also undertakes the procurement of supplies for the departments of the GoS. The organisation has broken even. SIMFED procures items such as fertilizers, livestock feeds, seeds, pesticides, agricultural implements uniforms, cement, misc. items, consumer goods and agricultural surplus marketing.

Remarks

The organization lacks continuity of purpose and management. The organization is characterised by lack of managerial skills, infrastructure, working capital and adequate stock-in-trade. It has failed to act as a price leader in regard to product in which it trades. The Federation duplicates its activities with STC, Denjong, and Sikkim Consumer Co-operative Society.

Restructuring Cost

- *Low working capital base*: Working capital base of SIMFED is very meager in comparison to its proposed plans of business. Capital inducted by the government considering earlier shape of business is not sufficient to carry its overall business. SIMFED is doing other business in order to meet its operative expenses.
- *Lack of infrastructure*: it may be mentioned here that SIMFED does not possess any building of its own and it operates in rental premises in all part of the state. The rent paid for the premises is inflating the total expenditure of the federation. Many of the expansion and diversification of activities of SIMFED is hindered for want of adequate and suitable premises and corresponding rent to be paid to the owner of house building. Recently, we are on the move to own a plot of land at Tadong for construction of office cum central godown.
- *Upgradation of working standard*: The activities of SIMFED are increasing day by day and the modern facilities to

undertake such activities are needed for the federation. These include computerization of accounting system, purchases and sales system and other allied activities on par with other institution. Computerization minimizes time taken for processing different proposal and also for preparing the things in the systematic manner.

- *Poor status of affiliated member societies*: SIMFED is supposed to carry out its marketing activities with its affiliated member societies. They are the main link between SIMFED and farmers. Our link with farmers located throughout the State is only through them. But in reality, most of these societies are financially unsound and cash-trapped one. They are poor business planner for which we need to support them with all kinds of infrastructural facilities. To make grassroots level societies more effective, indirect financial packages has to be arranged which may also include technical support like field level training to the Multipurpose Co-operative Societies (MPCS) functionaries.
- *Diversification of activities*: Though established with main objectives to take active part in marketing of agricultural produce and other agro-processing activities and marketing of consumer foods thereby involvement in manufacturing of consumer house hold goods, so far, we could not initiate any positive effort in this line which may be due to so many associated factors such as location, topography, availability of raw material, home market base etc.
- Situation could temporarily evade with involvement I Departmental supply works with support of Government to sustain affairs of SIMFED. Now time has come to start thinking towards the real objectives for which SIMFED has been created. In this line the following tentative projects have been selected for necessary implementation. They are:

— Establishment of collection cum marketing centers for surplus agricultural produces (SAP) marketing;
— Established of three marketing outlet for wholesale consumer business;
— Manufacturing unit of Exercise note books;

- Marketing of cut flowers;
- Obtaining carrying and forwarding agency or sole distributorship for the entire state for any of the product which could generate the profit for its own sustenance.

Particulars	*Amt (Rs in crore)*
Working Capital assistance to diversify the business sector as per its Bye laws and to enter into manufacturing activities	Rs 10.00
Cost of construction of four nos. of collection centers cum godowns and its sales/showrooms in different places of the States	Rs 5.00
Infrastructure developments for marketing of cut flower viz. collection center and refrigerated van	Rs 1.00
Civil cost of construction of SIMFED 's office cum central godown at 5th mile Tadong	Rs 1.00
Establishment cost of Ex-book manufacturing unit	Rs 1.00
Writing off of bad debts and sundry debtors	Rs 1.00
Support to ease burden of IT & TOT and other taxes	Rs 0.50
Support for VRS scheme	Rs 0.50
Support to its affiliated member societies to give them indirect financial package and to impart training to manage the societies for at least first five years @Rs 1.00 lakh for 166 mpcs and 25 ccs = 191 socities	Rs 9.55
Security deposits and other formalities while obtaining dealership cum distributorship of various companies	Rs 0.10
Total	29.65

Suggested Restructuring

The corporation could be merged with STC. It could be allowed to renovate its plant and machinery. The financial support for required IT hardware and software could be considered for the corporation. The Federation could be merged into a broader entity combining SIMFED and Denjong Agricultural Co-operative Society.

Action Plan

- Valuation of Assets and Liabilities
- Diversification of activities proposed by setting up Ginger processing plant, cardimum processing plant, promoting corporative tourism, setting up of corporate manufacturing unit and obtaining C&F of big manufacturers for the state

- Conduct open auctions for cardimum
- Preparation of a corporate plan
- Complete merger activities into the proposed new entity combining Denjong and Sikkim Consumer Co-operative Society.
- Legal, accounting and financial preparation for merger into the proposed composite entity

Time Frame

The total restructuring should be completed in 1 year.

Name of the SLPE	: **Sikkim Power Development Corporation (SPDC)**
Date of incorporation	: 15th December 1978
Classification	: Utility
Administrative Dep.	: Department of Energy and Power, GoS.
No. of Employees	: 21
Total Investment	: Rs 53.01 crore
Accumulated losses	: –
Dividends	: Nil
Restructuring Path	: Closure or Liquidation or total divestiture
Anticipated Benefits	: Saving of Govt. Resources

Enterprise Profile

It is involved in the preparation of pre-feasibility report and detailed project reports of hydro-electric projects. It was also mandated to generate hydro energy. It has 21 employees on rolls of which 7 are managerial personnel. It has an equity investment of Rs 3.80 crore and long-term debt of Rs 50.01 crore. The debt bears the gurantee of the GoS. The corporation has not taken up any hydro energy generation project. The corporation lacks clarity about its vision and mission. SPDC has been toying with the idea of taking up generation schemes of about 100 mw if the government provides it a share capital of Rs 150 crore over a period of 4-5 years.

Remarks

The corporation has not taken off in terms of its work activities and the government is also not keen on its continuation

Suggested Restructuring

The corporation should be privatised/wound up.

Action Plan

- The assets and liabilities of the corporation should be valued and surrendered to the Energy and Power Department.
- VR to the existing employees be offered and those who are on deputation could be re-patriated to their parent departments.
- A consultant may be appointed to suggest the modalities of privatisation/closure.

Time Frame

To be wound up in three months.

Name of the SLPE	: **Sikkim Nationalised Transport (SNT)**
Date of incorporation	: 1944
Classification	: Utility sector
Administrative Dep.	: Department of Transport, GoS.
No. of Employees	: 824
Total Investment	: Rs 34.39 crore
Accumulated losses	: –
Dividends	: Nil
Restructuring Path	: Continue in the state sector with increased accent on resource mobilisation and profitability
Anticipated Benefits	: Improved fulfilment of public purpose
Valuation	: Rs 1.19 crore
Restructuring Cost	: Rs 40.60 crore

Enterprise Profile

There was no public transportation system in Sikkim till 1944 when a Truck Department was created which was subsequently renamed Sikkim Nationalised Transport (SNT) in 1955. As most of the routes within the State were nationalised prior to 1975, all passengers and goods were exclusively transported by SNT buses and trucks or under its supervision. However, the system has been diluted after the extension of the Central Motor Vehicle Act, 1988 to Sikkim. Nevertheless, the bulk of passengers and the goods traffic in the State are still being carried by SNT *(See: Govt. of Sikkim, Report of the Comptroller and Auditor General of India, March 2003, p 24)*. SNT has 12 depots-cum-ticket booking officers for buses within the State one at Siliguri (West Bengal). In addition, there are four ticket booking agents at other places within the State and one at Kalimpong (West Bengal). SNT also operates three depots for trucks at Gangtok, Rangpo and Jorethang. It has one Central Workshop at Jalipool for major repairs and workshops at Gangtok, Rangpo, Jorethang and Rhenock for minor repairs. It has 100 buses, 54 trucks and 38 tankers. Its total fleet strength is 192.

Organisational Setup

The chart shows that the concept of line and staff is followed in the SNT. The concept has become outdated. The transport sector enterprises follow the SBU approach in organising their activities. The functions such as R&D, job evaluation, performance measurements, training and management development, resource raising and bench marking find no place in the organisaitonal chart.

Organizational Chart

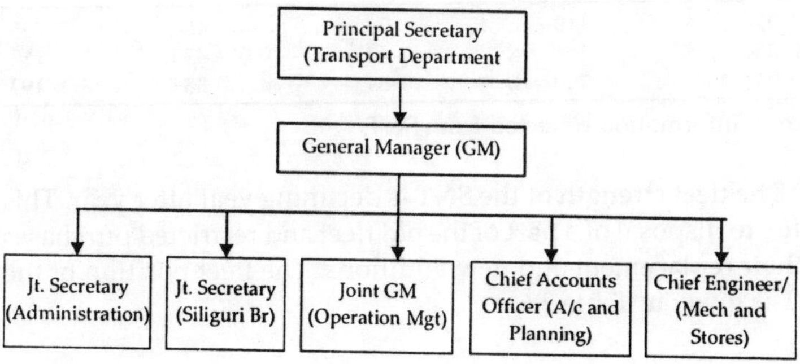

Financial Position and the Working Results

Table 5.5 shows SNT has been a loss making organization. However, the operating deficit has been decline over the years in terms percentage to revenue earned. It is interesting to note that SNTs revenue from hire charges have been more as compared to revenue from its trucks and tankers.

Table 5.5: Financial Position and the working results

(Rs. in crore)

Particulars	*1998-99*	*1999-00*	*2001-02*	*2002-03*	*2003-04*
Operating Revenue	**9.53**	**10.10**	**11.91**	**15.41**	**17.46**
Passenger traffic	1.36	1.66	2.39	2.18	1.68
Goods traffic	4.50	4.76	4.65	8.13	10.42
Sale of POL	3.56	3.61	4.56	4.78	5.12
Miscellaneous	0.11	0.07	0.31	0.32	0.24
Oprating Expenses	**17.92**	**20.38**	**19.47**	**22.49**	**22.15**
Passenger traffic	12.03	12.73	12.63	16.32	16.38
Goods traffic					
Purchase of POL	5.43	6.99	6.24	5.40	5.07
Miscellaneous	0.46	0.66	0.60	0.77	0.70
Operating deficit	–8.39	–10.28	–7.56	–7.08	–4.69
Percentage of deficit to revenue	**88**	**102**	**63**	**46**	**27**

Source: Information collected from SNT.

Fleet Strength

Table 5.6 depicts the fleet strength of the SNT.

Table 5.5: Fleet Strength

Year	*Bus*	*Truck*	*Tanker*	*Total*
2001-02	110	70	45	225
2002-03	106	63	43	212
2003-04	100	54	38	192

Source: Information collected from SNT.

The fleet strength of the SNT is declining year after year. This is due to disposal of a part of the old fleet and restricted purchases as their replacement and new additions. The fleet position of the SNT is given in Table 5.6.

Acquisition of the Fleet

During the period 2001-02 to 2003-04, 64 vehicles were disposed off. Against these numbers of disposed vehicles only 22 new vehicles were inducted in the fleet for the entire 3 years period. The ARSTU norms state that atleast 60 per cent of the fleet strength should be comprised of vehicles not less than 4 years old. The present percentage of such vehicles of SNT is a mere 19.68 per cent which is way below the prescribed ARSTU norm. The vehicle to staff ratio of the Department is around 4, which is well above the national average of 2.51 per cent. The department has to have the fleet augmented in order to break even and generate profits:

Trucks 20 × 8.00 lakhs	160.00
Tankers 5 × 10.00 lakhs	50.00
Mini Buses 5 × 5.00 lakhs	25.00
	235.00

Acquisition of Fleet

Financial Year	*No. of vehicles disposed off*	*No. of vehicle inducted in the fleet*	*Short[illegible]*
2001-02	Buses-9 Trucks-13 Total 22	Buses-5 Trucks-6 Total 11	Buses-4 Trucks-7 Total 11
2002-03	Buses-8 Trucks-12 Tankers-2 Total 22	Buses-4 Trucks-5 Total 9	Buses-4 Trucks-7 Total 2
2003-04	Buses-6 Tankers-5 Trucks-9 Total 20	Buses- Trucks-2 Total 2	Buses-6 Tankers-5 Trucks-7 Total 18

Source: Information collected from SNT.

Fleet Utilisation

Fleet utilisation is the ratio of the vehicles on road to the average number of vehicles held. According to the recommendation of the

Association of State Road Transport Undertakings (ASRTU), 92 per cent of the fleet should be road worthy of which 90 per cent shall kept in operation and 2 per cent as reserve. In respect of buses, the fleet utilisation of SNT ranged between 75 to 85 per cent during 1998-99 to 2002-03, falling short of the norm by 7 to 17 per cent. The fleet utilisaiton of trucks ranged between 70 to 95 per cent during 1998-99 to 2002-03

Vehicle Productivity (VP)

The vehicle productivity indicates the average revenue earning kilometer covered by each vehicle per day, for which SNT had not fixed any norm. The VP of SNT buses for the period 1998-99 to 2000-01 compared with that of other hill State's Road Transport Corporation RTC are shown in Table 5.7 below:

Table 5.7: Vehicle Productivity in Road Transport Corp in North East

State Road Transport Corp.	*1998-99*	*1999-00*	*2001-01*
SNT	85.64	81.90	80.72
Himachal RTC	215.10	224.80	223.40
Meghalaya RTC	186.10	121.10	136.90
Nagaland RTC	–	103.90	132.50
Mizoram RTC	118.40	119.60	118.80
All India Average	279.00	295.00	267.00

Source: Govt. of Sikkim, Report of the Comptroller and Auditor General of India, March 03.

Operational Efficiency

According to the latest fare formula of SNT adopted with effect from Feb 2002, the expenditure per kilometer per bus worked out to Rs 20.02 and RS 18.74. Out of 9,638 bus trips operated out of Gangtok during 2002-03, in 2,923 and 6,715 long and short distance trips respectively the per kilometer earnings per bus was less than the cost. The loss on this account worked out to Rs 1.17 crore during 2002-03 for Gangtok depot alone.

It was also seen that SNT discontinued services, reasons for which were not record, from Gangtok, to Pelling and District Courts from August 2000 and September 2002 even though these services recorded high average earning of Rs 33.78 and Rs 27.99

per kilometer. SNT resumed the Pelling service form October 2000 to November 2000 during which period the average earning came down to Rs 7.23 per kilometer. Thereafter, this service was discontinued.

Fuel Efficiency

SNT had fixed efficiency of buses at three kilometers per liter of HSD. However, the actual consumption was 1.82 kmpl, 2.19 kmpl, 1.88 kmpl, and 1.82 kmpl. The extra expenditure on HSD incurred by SNT due to the lower fuel efficiency being 27 to 37 per cent less than the norm and the consequent adverse impact on its profitability, SNT did not consider it necessary even once during the period under review to ascertain the reasons or take remedial measures. Further, the fuel efficiency of SNT buses for the period 1998-02 was the lowest compared to the Road Transport Corp. of other states with topographies similar to Sikkim, as evident from the table 5.8 below:

Table 5.8: Fuel Efficiency

State Road Transport Corp.	*1998-99*	*1999-00*	*2001-02*	*2002-03*
SNT	1.82	2.41	2.19	1.88
Meghalaya RTC	3.19	3.11	3.17	NA
Nagaland RTC	NA	3.50	3.50	3.50
Mizoram RTC	3.00	3.00	2.87	2.74
All India Average	3.68	3.67	3.53	4.59

Source: Govt. of Sikkim, Report of the Comptroller and Auditor General of India, March 2003.

Strengths, Weaknesses, Opportunities and Threats (SWOT) Analysis

Strengths

The time proven strength of the department is that it has consistently achieved its revenue as well as social obligations. In the last Financial Year 2004-05 alone, against the Government target of Rs. 21.50 crore the department not only achieved the target but also exceeded it by almost 8 crore.

- The existing law of land gives SNT the absolute transport

market on all the domestic routes as well as the NH 31 A as these are nationalized routes. In principle, what this means is that SNT is the only recognized public transporter for the State. Here it may be noted that even the private trucks carrying public commodities have to run under the supervision of SNT. It implies that legally SNT has 100 per cent control over the Transport business in the State of Sikkim.

- SNT has a very efficient and experienced work force both in the Operation Section as well as the mechanical section, which are the backbone of any transport organization. The department has also very good infrastructural setup like depots, workshops, godowns etc. all over the state as well as in the state of West Bengal.
- The SNT has fully established its Brand name over the years. The number of accidents and fatalities is almost nil in the case of SNT. SNT is the sole official carrier of both the passengers and goods of important organizations and departments as such the Army, General Reserve Engineering Force (GREF), all Oil Companies, FCI, all State government departments etc,

Weaknesses

- The main weakness of the department is that it has not been able to restructure its activities whereby the department has over the period of years lost the competitive edge to its competitors in private sector. Although, the freight business is almost 100 per cent with the department, it has lost considerable grip over the passenger sector mainly because of its inability to modernise passenger carrier sector.
- Proper Manpower planning and optimum utilization of the workforce needs a serious review as the financial burden of maintaining the excess manpower can not be continued for long.
- The main weakness of the department is that it has not been able to hold an optimum number of fleet. The department is totally dependent on the Government for the funds required for its augmentation of fleet. Against

the projected, optimum fleet of 400-500 vehicles the department has only 192 vehicles at its disposal.

- The present fleet of functional vehicles is over aged and consists of 66 per cent of vehicles, which are over 10 to 14 years old. This factor adversely affects the important parameters such as vehicle productivity, load factor, etc.

Opportunity

- SNT has a great scope to increase its market share. With the increase in the flow of tourists, its market share is expected to increase further. The setting up of hydro electric projects, helipads, airports and opening up of the Nathulla Pass is expected to brighten the scenario further.

Threats

- The shrinking fleet is the biggest threat. The over manning is also causing a great stress. Too tight a departmental control is obstructing innovativeness and depriving the SNT of a healthy corporate culture. The corporation has become the dumping ground of un-required personnel who lack professional knowledge. The department has no vision. It does not have a corporate plan.

The organisation caters to the transportation need of all government departments central agencies and general public. The organization has been entrusted by the responsibility of handling freight for army. The corporation provides bus services to every hamlet and town of the state. The occupancy rate is very low, the buss staff ratio is very high, the buses are out modeled, the fuel consumption is very high, the corporation has been incurring losses year after year. The fleet strength is depleting, the age profile is highly un-favourable. The organization faces a stiff competition from private bus operators. The services provided need vast improvement. The investment from the government is not forthcoming. The departmental form of running the organisation robs it of autonomy and puts a heavy burden of accountability. The fuel efficiency of the SNT buses was lower compared to the

Road Transport Corporations of other states with topographies similar to Sikkim. The vehicle productivity followed the same trend. The organization was characterized by access consumption of engine oil, wastage of burnt engine oil, loss due to sale of condemned vehicles with out tender process and shortage of stock material.

Remarks

There is a need to operate SNT in future too. The transport needs of the State would continue to grow. The private sector could co-exist. The social obligations in the transport sector could be fulfilled only by the SNT. However, SNT has to restructure its functioning.

Valuation

- *Land*: The total valuation of land alone belonging to SNT is estimated at Rs. 69.42 Cores.
- *Buildings*: SNT has well established office buildings, truck parking yards, guest-houses all over the state and at Siliguri, West Bengal. The net valuation of building alone is estimated at Rs, 15.36 crore.
- *Stocks*: The net fast moving consumable, like fuel, oil, spare parts in possession of the department at any given time is estimated at Rs. 3 crore.
- *Vehicles*: The present market valuation of the vehicles is estimated at Rs. 22 crore
- *Sundry Debtors*: The Sundry Debtors stand at Rs. 3.50 crore. This is the amount receivable from Army and Oil Companies.
- *Miscellaneous*: SNT has got substantial investment in plants and machinery in the various depots and workshops. The department also has major equipments or units such as Weighbridges (3 nos.), tyre rethreading plant, petrol pumps. The net valuation of these plants and machinery along with the total office equipments is estimated at Rs. 6.05 cores.

Valuation

Name of enterprise		*Land*	*Building*	*Stocks of Machinery, oil, fuel etc*	*Vehicles (Functioning and non-functioning*	*Sundry Debtors*	*Others*	*Total*
SNT Transport Department	Jorethang	12.00	01.40					
	Siliguri	20.00	05.00				Plant and Machinery 03.00	
	Gangtok	27.00	06.00				Office Equp. 02.00	
	Tadong	03.40	00.05				Pump 00.60	
	Rangpo	02.00	00.50				W. Bridge 00.45	
	Namchi	00.13	00.02					
	Mangan	00.80	00.04					
	Gyalsing	00.60	00.20					
	Melli	00.90	00.05					
	Jalipool	03.00	02.00					
	Rhenock	00.40	00.10					
Total		69.42	15.36	03.00	22.00	3.50	06.05	119.33

Restructuring Cost

- *Voluntary Retirement Scheme (VRS)*: With the onset of the VRS introduced by the Government 88 numbers of staff of SNT had applied for VRS through the recommendation of the department. However, due to fund constraint only the case of 8 persons was considered. We still have old applications of 80 persons seeking VRS and in addition it is estimated that a minimum of 30 more applicants could likely submit applications for VR. The net fund requirement on VR @ 8 lakhs on average works out to Rs. 880 lakhs.
- *Renovation and Expansion*: Many depots including both the workshops and booking offices of SNT need to be renovated to improve working environment. The depot wise fund requirement for the renovation of booking offices, truck parking yards workshops, etc., is estimated at Rs. 60 lakhs.
- *Upgradation of Plant and Machinery*: With the advent of modern technology, the present day vehicles are much more sophisticated and therefore the cost of up gradation of the plant and machinery is estimated at Rs. 30 lakhs.
- *IT Requirements*: In order to set-up an efficient system of reimbursement of freight bills, the maintenance of stock inventory etc. It is necessary to introduce computers. The cost of IT requirement including both hardware and software is estimated to Rs 10 lakhs.
- *Court Cases*: In variably, the nature of work is such that there will be court cases as result of accidents etc., the cost on accounts of this is estimate at Rs 10 lakhs.
- *Contingency Liability*: In order to take care of the unforeseen rise in the cost of the operations, a contingency of 4 per cent on the total sundry creditors is estimated at Rs 8 lakhs.
- *Operational Deficit*: In spite of exceeding the revenue target, the department has a operational deficit of 400 lakhs This is maily attributed to the fact that SNT being a department, in the interest of the general public, is obliged to maintain the operations of bus services in almost 29 uneconomical routes. The department also gives concessions to the students, senior citizenship, Ex-servicemen etc. Primary

reason for deficit is that the department is excessively overstaffed whereby the present expenditure on salaries and wages alone exceeds 10 crores per annum. Therefore, the cost of restructuring cost in order to compensate the operational deficit i5 estimated at Rs. 400 lakhs.

- *Advertisement and Promotion*: The department needs to promote and advertise. Its businesses and activities so as to reach a larger section of the people. The restructuring cost on account of advertisement and promotion is estimated at Rs. 10 lakhs.
- *Sundry Creditors*: The restructuring cost on account of Sundry Creditors is estimated at Rs. 200 lakhs.
- *Acquisition of Fleet*: Perhaps, the most important action that the department has to take immediately is to augment its fleet. The restructuring cost for acquisition of 50 buses, 125 trucks and 25 nos. of tankers is estimated at Rs. 2237 lakhs.
- *Spare Parts*: The department needs to stock adequate quantities of spare parts. The restructuring cost for the requirement of spare parts is estimated at Rs. 2 crore.

Restructuring Process

Restructuring SNT involves marketing, human resource, finances, commercial, material, workshops, operations, schedules and overall organisational change management. The restructured organisation has to cope with the changing market needs, achieve the business goals and make the corporate vision a reality. Vision, mission and passion to excel must become the watchwords of a new work culture. A strategic approach is suggested under each of the important aspects of the restructuring plan.

Marketing Restructuring

- Expand capacities to service all District Headquarters and neighboring State capital cities.
- Broaden service facilities by way of Ordinary, Fast Service, Express, Luxury, Hi-Tech buses with different fare/stage structures to suit various needs and sections of the population.

Restructuring Costs

(Rs. in crore)

VRS	*Training*	*Renovation/ Expansion*	*IT Requirement*	*Contingent liability*	*Operational deficit*	*Advertisement*	*Sun. Creditors*	*Acquisition of fleet 200 nos. fleet*	*Forecast needs of spares for optimum fleet*	*Total*
80 Old + 30 New X 8 lakhs = 8.80		Jrt 0.65						Bus-50 Rs @ 13.08 = 654.00 lakh Trucks 125 Rs @ 10.52 = 1315.00 lakh Tanker 25 Rs @10.72 = 268.00 lakh		
		Sng 0.40 Rpo 0.50 Jpl 0.14 Gtk 0.20 Nam 0.10								
8.80	0.15	0.90 (includes upgradations of Rs 0.30 crore)	0.10	0.08	4.00	0.10	2.00	22.37	2.00	40. 60

- Strive for customer/passenger satisfaction by improving safety, regularity and punctuality of services.
- Tie up with Tourism Corporation/other public undertakings and meet their transport needs.
- Introduce Booking Agencies at all important traffic points.
- Organise regular traffic/opinion surveys to identify profitable routes.
- Conduct regular opinion surveys to refine operations to secure better passenger satisfaction.
- Introduction of marriage, personal, excursion tours to fill idle time of spare vehicles.
- Introduction of "Transport Cards".

Financial Restructuring

- Identify low cost fund sources.
- Reduce interest liabilities.
- Conversion of State/Central Government loans as equity.
- Conversion of interest due to State and Central Government as equity.
- Clearance of loans/interests of Finance Institutions/Banks by obtaining low cost funds.
- Rationalisation of MV tax system to improve operational viability.
- Waiver of MV taxes due to the State Government to set off the cost of services rendered by the Corporation by way of travel concession.
- Depreciation Fund provision of Rs.20.00 lakhs may be waived.
- Rationalisation of internal accounts and audit system
- Obtain grants and budgeted subsidies from State Government towards bus pass concessions.

Human Resource Restructuring

- Lay down norms of staffing and reduce unproductive supporting staff.
- Improve the employee productivity by deploying required crew.
- Introduction of inter-functional transferability of supporting staff categories to Drivers/Conductors.

- Payment of employees' terminal benefits.
- Introduction of suitable VRS and offer to all willing supporting staff.
- Introduction of structured managerial and supervisory development training programmes for updating skills.
- Effective implementation of MOU system.
- Strengthening good employee-relation schemes.
- Introduction of suitable incentive schemes for all employees.

Commercial Restructuring

- Leasing and renting of Corporation infrastructure.
- Introduction of advertisements on bus stations, buses, bus shelters, tickets, CTV advertisement, etc.
- Introduction of parcel and courier services through Corporation buses.
- Maximise luggage revenues i.e. accompanied as well as unaccompanied luggage.
- Maximise the revenue on postal services.
- Maximise the revenue on paper parcel service.

Material Management Restructuring

- Introduction of integrated material management systems.
- Stocking of Depot spares inventory at 4 Zonal Headquarters.
- Standardizing stocking of spare parts with rationalized minimum and maximum limits as per the consumption pattern in order to reduce inventory carrying cost.
- Rationalisation of purchase policies to reduce inventory.
- Rationalisation of standardisation of disposal/auction activities of vehicles, scrap, tyres, batteries, etc.
- Tie up with oil companies to secure petrol, oil and lubricants (POL) at reasonable rates.

Operational Restructuring

- Scheduling of buses with minimum inputs of bus and crew for given traffic demand and design cost-effective transport systems.

- Structuring of operations with optimum service mix to have better return.
- Rationalisation of ticket system as per the service mix.
- Standardizations of various types of services with different stage structures.
- Rationalisation of fare structure.
- Identification of threats from competitors on each route and formulate strategies for effective encounter.
- Identification of opportunities in terms of change of timings, permit variations, etc.
- Strengthening of bus station management.
- Strengthening of quality of services by improving safety, regularity and punctual operations. Creation of passenger relation cells. xi) Strengthening passenger information system.
- Introduction of privately hired buses to improve profitability.
- Augmentation of services on all high density routes.
- Rescheduling of low density and vehicle utilisation services.
- Introduction of services on all approved routes.
- Take advantage of route pattern as 71 per cent routes have length of more than 100 km.
- Strengthening of all inter-state routes.
- Restructuring 20 approved routes which have overlaps ranging from 5 to 56 km.
- Introduction of Hi-Tech buses to all District Headquarters with modern facilities.

Organisational Restructuring

- Smartsizing of Corporate Office with minimum staff. A lean Corporate Office is recommended.
- Closing of all Regional and Central Workshops to reduce cost of operation on workshop repairs.
- Abolition of all Divisional and Sub-Depots to minimise the personnel cost on not very productive offices and staff.
- Creation of 4 self-contained near autonomous operational zones with appropriate delegation of powers.
- Establishing a strong one-tier system controlled by Zonal

Office with supporting functions governed by federal administration from Corporate Office.

- Grouping of homogeneous functions to bring about economy.

Management Information Systems Restructuring

- Introduction of effective management information systems.
- Regular monitoring of Critical Successful Factors (CSF) to improve overall performance.
- Regular and timely exchange of information on few vital areas to focus managers' attention and bring about competitive spirit.
- Introduction of performance appraisal and review system.
- Introduction of computers.

Vehicle Maintenance Restructuring

- Introduction of preventive and breakdown maintenance systems.
- Enforcement of sound replacement policy.
- Strengthening of maintenance-operational systems and monitoring.
- Creation of Zonal Maintenance Engineers for this purpose.
- Introduction of technical, managerial and operational controls for fuel to improve use efficiency and performance.
- Introduction of technical controls in the area of tyres, lubes, batteries, springs, etc., to reduce the cost of operations.
- Scrapping of all vehicles over ten years age.
- Repairing of all vehicles which are less than ten years age.
- Auction of 6 Eicher vehicles.
- Rationalisation of fleet by making Bhopal, Indore as Leyland Comet bus and Jabalpur-Raipur as Tata bus zones.

Restructuring of Workshops

- Abolition of all Regional Workshops and Central Workshops to reduce Workshop repair costs.

- Establishment of Body Building Unit at Gwalior along with Printing Press and Training College.
- Establishment of four Zonal Workshops Co-terminus with Zonal Operational Units along with Tyre Retreading Shop and Training Schools,.
- Control of Body Building Unit and Training College to be vested in Corporate Office.
- Modernisation of Zonal Workshop Body Building units with latest machinery.

Suggested Restructuring

There is a need to corporatise SNT on a top priority basis. The organisaiton should be restructured around the SBU concept. Excess manpower should be given VR. New rules of human resource development, financial management, marketing management should find place in the organisation. The operational restructuring should be undertaken on war footing basis.

Action Plan

- Preparation of a corporate plan
- *Operational restructuring*: Renewal of fleet, re-organization of workshops, rethinking about the depots, acquisition of small sized buses to counter competition from private sector
- *Human resources restructuring*: Rightsizing the corporation, abolition of practices of appointing handy boy, stopping the appointment of un-required personnel from government, management development and training, higher personnel productivity, induction of professionals.
- *Financial restructuring*: Cost control and cost reduction, introduction of internal audit, low costs funding, fare revision and better cash flow management,
- *Technological restructuring*: Computerisation and GIS.

Time Frame

2-3 years for restructuring

Name of the SLPE	: **Sikkim Energy and Department of Power**
Date of incorporation	: 1967
Classification	: Utility sector
Administrative Dep.	: Department of Energy and Power, GoS
No. of Employees	: 3443
Total Investment	: Rs 514.79
Accumulated losses	: –
Dividends	: Nil
Restructuring Path	: Continue in the state sector with increased accent on resource mobilisation and profitability
Anticipated Benefits	: Improved fulfilment of public purpose

Enterprise Profile

The Sikkim Energy and Department of Power is involved in generating, transmitting, distributing and regulating power in the State of Sikkim. The total generation of power in Sikkim during 2004-05 was 45.96 million units. The central and other utilities had the generating capacity of 51.00 million units. The total capacity was 97 million units. It is expected that the total capacity will go up to 469 million units during 2011-12. The financial position of the power sector is extremely unhealthy due to high losses incurred, very high T& D losses (of approximately 51 per cent), excessive manpower, and very high distribution costs. The number of employees with the department per million KwH sold varied from 8.01 to 12.16 compared to the all India average of 2.6 to 3.25. The number of employees per thousand consumers in the case of the Department varied from 21.11 to 23.36 against the all India average between 7.78 and 9.89. The excess staffing not only resulted in increasing the cost of power but also contributed to the operating losses incurred by the Department year after year. The lack of clarity with regard to the policy for power sector is also acted as a major deterrent to the growth of power sector. The State of Sikkim has to fall in line with the central policy of power sector reforms. It has to unbundle the activities of the Energy and Department of Power and constitute separate entities for generation, transmission, distribution and regulation.

Remarks

The development of energy and power sector is the top priority for the State of Sikkim which has tremendous hydel resources. However, the sector can grow on the basis of vigorous participation of private sector.

Suggested Restructuring

The sector needs to be corporatised and then subsequently privatise in line with the present policy of the Government of India. There is a need to unbundeling the power sector into generation, transmission, distribution and regulatory entities. There is also a need to restructure the financial, commercial and human resources elements. This has been discussed in the study on Power Sector in Sikkim undertaken by the Administrative Staff College of India.

Action Plan

- Preparation of a corporate plan
- Unbundling the power sector into generation, transmission, distribution and regulatory entities.
- VR to excess employees
- Social Safety Net
- Financial, commercial and human resources related re-engineering
- Followup of 2003 Electricity Supply Act
- All other suggestions made in the ASCI Study as accepted by the GoS.

Time frame

As suggested in ASCI Study and accepted by the GoS.

Name of the SLPE	:	**Sikkim Scheduled Castes, Scheduled Tribes and Other Backward Classes Development Corporation (SABCCO)**
Date of incorporation	:	27th February 1996
Classification	:	
Administrative Dep.	:	Welfare Department, GoS.

No. of Employees	:	16
Total Investment	:	Rs 21.50 crore
Accumulated losses	:	Rs –1.69 crore
Dividends	:	Nil
Restructuring Path	:	Disinvest
Anticipated Benefits	:	Additional resource to Govt.
Valuation	:	Rs 1.43 crore
Restructuring Cost	:	Rs 6.00 crore

Enterprise Profile

The organisation has an authorized share capital of Rs 10 crore. It is a State Chanalising Agency which awaits financial assistance by way of loan from the Apex Corporation's at the national level viz., National Scheduled Tribes Finance Development Corporation and National Backward Classes Finance and Development Corporation for financing income generation schemes for the STs, SCs, OBCs and handicapped persons. The corporation was setup to: promote economic and development activities for the benefit of SC, ST, Other BC and handicapped persons; assist individuals or groups of individuals belonging to SC, ST, OBC and handicapped persons by way of loans and advances for income and employment generating activities; extend loans to SC, ST, OBC and handicapped persons for pursuing general/professional/technical education or training; help in furthering Government policies and programmes for the development of SC, ST, OBC and handicapped persons; enter into any agreement with Central Government/State Government or any State or Local authorities or otherwise for the purpose of carrying out objects of the Company; and obtain from any such Government, State authorities or persons any charters, subsidies, loans, grants, etc. The corporation provides term loan and micro credit to those involved in agriculture and allied operations, artisans, traditional occupation, technical trades, small business and hospitality industry.

Remarks

The enterprise is high on social purpose and resource mobilization. It incurs losses in the conduct of its business. It deals with the upliftment of STs, SCs, OBCs and handicapped persons. The organisation faces the problems of recoveries, delayed release of share capital from the government, and age old loans. The lack of an effective MIS is also impeding the functioning of the enterprise. It has very poor net working with the all-India institutions dealing with STs, SCs, OBCs and handicapped persons. The managerial personnel are untrained. The non-managerial personnel are not well versed with the functioning of welfare enterprises. The middle management is conspicuous by its absence.

Restructuring Cost

Restructuring Cost		*Amt (Rs in crore)*
1.	Grant in Aid for meeting administrative expenses	1.20
2.	Training for officers and staff-capacity building	0.10
3.	Computerisation—development loan software packages networking facilities to be provided, setup MIS cell	0.10
4.	Setting-up retail outlets in all four districts for displaying and selling items/products manufactured by SABCCO beneficiaries	0.15
5.	Write up provisions for bad and doubtful debts	1.50
6.	Provide funds for meeting the 1 per cent commission fee paid to state government for providing block government guarantee of Rs 25 core to Apex Corporations National Schedule Caste Finance Development Corporation (NSFDC), National Schedule Tribes Finance Development Corporation (NSTFDC), National Backward Class Finance Development Corporation (NBCFDC)	0.25
7.	Funds for promotional activities such as organising EDPs, awareness camps, advertisement and publicity.	0.25
8.	Provision for downsizing the manpower requirement	0.50
9.	Cost of conducting an evaluation study for a financial restructuring	0.50
10.	Cost of constructing and independent office building	1.00
	Total funds required as grant in aid	6.00

Suggested Restructuring

The enterprise should introduce OPTIMA and get networked with the national apex organisation. The organisational, financial and manpower restructuring should be taken up in the case of the enterprise.

Action Plan

- Preparation of a corporate plan
- Preparation of a blue print for financial restructuring
- Designing and implementing VRS scheme
- Induction of qualified professional
- Conduct of surveys of beneficiaries
- Installation of an MIS system
- Install adequate software and hardware
- Develop relationships with the national organisations
- Concentrate on micro finance
- Networking with national organisations
- Promoting schemes relating to micro-finance

Time Frame

Total restructuring should be completed with in six months.

Annexures

ANNEXURE 1.1

PROFILE OF SLPEs IN SIKKIM IN 2001-02

(Rs in Crore)

Name of the Enterprise	Establishment	Typology	Classification	Equity	Debt	Investment	Net Profit/ losses	Reserves	Accumulated Loss/Profit	Turnover	Net Worth	Capital Employed	Contribution
SIDICO	1977	Government Company	Financial	16.04	3.42	19.46	0.15	2.14	–10.34	1.19	7.84	21.6	0.17
State Bank of Sikkim	1968	Public Corporation	Financial	0.58	3.98	4.56	–1.85	9.48	–23.26	9.54	0	10.06	2.38
Sikkim State Co-operative Bank	1998	Co-operative society	Financial	8.5	0	8.50	i.09	0.6	1.1	1.76	0	22.36	0
Sikkim Jewels	1972	Government Company	Manufacturing	5.49	1.61	7.10	–0.06	0.86	0.62	2.26	6.19	4.72	0.06
Sikkim Hatchery	1994	Government Company	Manufacturing	0.46	0	0.46	0	0	0	1.2	0	0	0
Sikkim Poultry	1999	Government Company	Manufacturing	0.79	0	0.79	–0.02	–0.11	–0.26	0	0.53	0.54	0
Sikkim Precision Industries	1999	Government Company	Manufacturing	0	0	0.00	0	0	0	0	0	0	0
SITCO	1976	Government Company	Manufacturing	10.97	0.99	11.96	–0.51	5.47	–5.11	4.86	12.27	11.31	1.53
Tea Board of Sikkim	1974	Public Corporation	Manufacturing	19.52	0	19.52	0.08	0	8.04	2.01	7.91	8.54	0.16
Sikkim Milk Union	1980	Co-operative society	Manufacturing	0.02	0.08	0.10	–0.75	2.67	–1.22	4.39	1.41	–0.4	–0.26
Govt. Fruit Preservation Factory	1964	Government Company	Manufacturing	0	0	0.76	0.05	0	0.11	1.31	0.75	1.96	0
Sikkim Tourism	1998	Government Company	Promotional	4.79	0	4.79	0.67	0	0	1.3	4.84	1.45	0.43

(Contd.)

ANNEXURE 1.1: (Contd.)

Name of the Enterprise	Establishment	Typology	Classification	Equity	Debt	Investment	Net Profit/ losses	Reserves	Accumulated Loss/Profit	Turnover	Net Worth	Capital Employed	Contribution
Sikkim Handloom and Handicrafts Dev. Corp. Ltd	2003	Government Company	Promotional	0	0	0	0	0	0	0	0	0	—
Khadi and Village Board	1978	Public Corporation	Promotional	0	0.34	10.09	–0.21	0	0	0.16	0	0	0
State Trading Corp.	1972	Public Corporation	Trade and Service	1.11	0	1.11	0.75	4.21	4.21	12.93	4.8	5.32	0
Sikkim Consumer Co-operative Soceity	1975	Co-operative society	Trade and Service	0.17	0	0.17	0.009	0.19	0.61	2.04	0.46	0	2.02
SIMFED	1982	Co-operative society	Trade and Service	0.88	0.17	1.05	0.32	1.28	–0.22	15.01	2.17	0	0.71
Denjong	1965	Co-operative society	Trade and Service	0.2	0	0.20	–0.42	0.19	–0.25	6.09	1.13	0.17	0.02
Sikkim National Transport Corp.	1944	Departmental Enterprise	Utility	33.08	0	33.08	–3.74	–6.4	0	15.41	0	0	0
State Energy and Department of Power	1967	Departmental Enterprise	Utility	470.92	0	470.92	–65.85	0	0	11.85	0	0	0
Sikkim Power Dev. Corp.	1998	Government Company	Utility	3	50.01	53.01	0	0	0	0	2.4	3.19	0
SABCCO	1996	Government Company	Welfare	6.49	9.12	15.61	0.35	0	–0.16	0.69	6.14	0	–0.32

0 – Data not existing/available.

Source: Annexure 1.9.

ANNEXURE 1.2

PROFILE OF SLPEs IN SIKKIM IN 2002-03

(Rs. in Crore)

Name of the Enterprise	Establishment	Typology	Classification	Equity	Debt	Investment	Net Profit/ losses	Reserves	Accumulated loss/ profit	Turnover	Net Worth	Capital Employed	Contribution
SIDICO	1977	Government Company	Financial	16.54	2.94	19.48	2.51	2.4	–7.83	3.45	11.11	21.88	2.53
State Bank of Sikkim	1968	Public Corporation	Financial	0.58	4.4	4.98	–21.57	9.48	–44.84	12.08	0	10.06	5.15
Sikkim State Co-operative Bank	1998	Co-operative society	Financial	8.91	0	8.91	0.23	1.47	0.35	1.78	0	241.4	0
Sikkim Jewels	1972	Government Company	Manufacturing	5.99	1.83	7.82	0.05	1.65	0.66	2.15	7.51	5.36	0.01
Sikkim Hatchery	1994	Government Company	Manufacturing	0	0	0.46	0	0	0	1.38	0	0	0
Sikkim Poultry	1999	Government Company	Manufacturing	0	0	0.79	–0.11	–0.08	–0.34	0	0.45	0.45	0
Sikkim Precision Industries	1999	Government Company	Manufacturing	3.7	0	3.70	0.12	0	0.12	0.4	3.82	0	0
SITCO	1976	Government Company	Manufacturing	11.22	0.81	12.03	–2.68	2.63	2.26	2.96	9.7	8.07	–0.52
Tea Board of Sikkim	1974	Public Corporation	Manufacturing	20.44	0	20.44	–0.22	0	7.82	1.75	7.84	8.38	0.9
Sikkim Milk Union	1980	Co-operative society	Manufacturing	0.06	0.08	0.14	–0.71	3.42	–1.67	4.54	1.72	–0.63	–0.11
Govt. Fruit Preservation Factory	1964	Government Company	Manufacturing	0	0	1.07	–0.06	0.09	0.4	0.17	1.79	2.04	0
Sikkim Tourism	1998	Government Company	Promotional	4.79	0	4.79	–0.96	0	–0.6	0.92	4.13	–0.96	0.08

(Contd.)

ANNEXURE 1.2: (Contd.)

Name of the Enterprise	Establishment	Typology	Classification	Equity	Debt	Investment	Net Profit/ losses	Reserves	Accumulated loss/ profit	Turnover	Net Worth	Capital Employed	Contribution
Sikkim Handloom and Handicrafts Dev. Corp. Ltd	2003	Government Company	Promotional	0	0	0	0	0	0	0	0	0	—
Khadi and Village Board	1978	Public Corporation	Promotional	10.89	0.35	11.24	–0.19	0	0	0.2	0	0	0.01
State Trading Corp.	1972	Public Corporation	Trade and Service	0	0	1.11	0.98	0	0	19.54	6.6	0	0
Sikkim Consumer Co-operative Soceity	1975	Co-operative society	Trade and Service	0.17	0	0.17	0.10	0.22	0.69	3.21	0.47	0	3.2
SIMFED	1982	Co-operative society	Trade and Service	0.84	0.17	1.01	0.15	1.37	–0.19	11.53	2.21	0	0.43
Denjong	1965	Co-operative society	Trade and Service	0.2	0	0.20	–0.34	0.19	–0.36	0.59	1.02	0.18	0.02
Sikkim National Transport Corp.	1944	Departmental Enterprise	Utility	34.49	0	34.49	–4.88	–4.97	0	17.39	0	0	0
State Energy and Department of Power	1967	Departmental Enterprise	Utility	470.92	0	470.92	–37.36	0	0	13.31	0	0	0
Sikkim Power Dev. Corp.	1998	Government Company	Utiltiy	3	50.01	53.01	0	0	0	0	3	8.39	0
SABCCO	1996	Government Company	Welfare	8.99	11.11	20.10	–1.12	0	–1.56	0.78	8.59	0	–0.36

0 – Data not existing/available.

Source: Annexure 1.9.

ANNEXURE 1.3

PROFILE OF SLPEs IN SIKKIM IN 2003-04

(Rs. in Crore)

Name of the Enterprise	Establish-ment	Typology	Classification	Equity	Debt	Invest-ment	Net Profit/ loses	Reserves	Accumu-lated loss/ profit	Turn-over	Net Worth	Capital Employed	Contrib ution
SIDICO	1977	Government Company	Financial	17.04	2.62	19.66	0.47	2.4	–7.36	1.73	12.08	22.06	—
State Bank of Sikkim	1968	Public Corporation	Financial	0.58	4.82	5.4	–0.95	0.11	–36.42	14.8	0	10.06	2.79
Sikkim State Co-operative Bank	1998	Co-operative society	Financial	9.36	0	9.36	0.69	0	1.05	2	0	27	0.7
Sikkim Jewels	1972	Government Company	Manufacturing	6.49	0.56	7.05	–0.38	1	0.28	2.05	7.65	4.82	2.21
Sikkim Hatchery	1994	Government Company	Manufacturing	0	0	0.46	0	—	0	1.38	0	0	0
Sikkim Poultry	1999	Government Company	Manufacturing	0	0	0.79	–0.08	—	0	0	0	0	0
Sikkim Precision Industries	1999	Government Company	Manufacturing	0	0	3.7	0.04	0.12	–0.02	0.33	3.87	0	0.4
SITCO	1976	Government Company	Manufacturing	11.22	0.52	11.74	–3.29	—	–2.92	2.39	4.54	–0.20	–1.2
Tea Board of Sikkim	1974	Public Corporation	Manufacturing	22.71	0	22.71	0.03	1.89	7.82	1.91	7.77	8.78	0.05
Sikkim Milk Producers Union	1980	Co-operative Society		0.06	0.08	0.14	–1.03	0	–2.54	4.22	0.85	–1.20	
Govt. Fruit Preservation Factory	1964	Government Company	Manufacturing	0	0	0	0.02	0.88	0.60	0.14	1.02	2.21	0.43
Sikkim Tourism	1998	Government Company	Promotional	6.06	0	6.06	–0.65	1.53	–2.59	1.34	–3.41	3.22	0.5
Sikkim Handloom and Handicrafts Dev. Corp. Ltd	2003	Government Company	Promotional	0.80	0	0.80	0	—	0.05	0.25	0.93	0	—
Khadi and Village Board	1978	Public Corporation	Promotional	11.66	0.35	12.01	0	—	0	0.14	0	0	—
State Trading Corp.	1972	Public Corporation	Trade and Service	0	0	1.11	0.66	0.74	0	15.53	7.9	0	1.13

(Contd.)

ANNEXURE 1.3: (Contd.)

Name of the Enterprise	Establishment	Typology	Classification	Equity	Debt	Investment	Net Profit/ loses	Reserves	Accumulated loss/ profit	Turnover	Net Worth	Capital Employed	Contribution
Sikkim Consumer Co-operative Society	1975	Co-operative society	Trade and Service	0.17	0	0.17	0.008	0.24	0.75	2.4	0.5	0	2.32
SIMFED	1982	Co-operative society	Trade and Service	1.02	0	1.02	0.19	—	0	16.94	0	0	—
Denjong	1965	Co-operative society	Trade and Service	0.2	0	0.2	–0.46	0.19	–0.83	6.1	0.94	0.19	0
Sikkim National Transport Corp.	1944	Departmental Enterprise	Utility	34.49	0	34.49	–4.2	0	0	17.24	0	0	–3.44
State Energy and Department of Power	1967	Departmental Enterprise	Utility	514.79	0	514.79	–22.69	0	0	13.57	0	0	0
Sikkim Power Dev. Corp.	1998	Government Company	Utility	3	50.01	53.01	0	—	0	0	3	6.86	—
SABCCO	1996	Government Company	Welfare	9.55	11.95	21.5	–1.12	–0.13	–1.69	0.93	9.42	0	–0.02

0 – Data not existing/available.

Source: Annexure 1.9.

ANNEXURE 1.4

OBJECTIVES OF SLPEs

SIDICO

1. To provide long-term loans for setting up cottage, tiny, small and medium industries also for expansion diversification and modernisation,
2. To provide financial assistance for Hotel industry, small hospitals/nursing homes,
3. To provide seed capital assistance towards promoter's contribution under the scheme of IDBI /SIDBI,
4. Participation in share capital for joint sector projects,
5. Disbursement of Central and State Government incentives,
6. Setting up and development of industrial areas and industrial estates; and,
7. Achieving rapid industrial and economic development of the state.

State Bank of Sikkim

1. To cater to the banking requirements by undertaking commercial lending, investment and treasury functions.

Sikkim State Co-operative Bank Ltd.

1. To serve as a balancing center for all co-operative societies in the state.
2. To raise deposits and share capital for giving loans to member co-operative societies and other individual members against viable schemes.
3. To do all type of banking business as defined in Sections 5 and 6(1) of the Banking Regulation Act 1949.

Sikkim Jewels Ltd.

1. Providing employment to locals.
2. Producing watch jewels, industrial jewels, rotor magnets, disposable syringes.

Sikkim Poultry Development Corp.

1. Promote, establish, administer, own and run, improve, develop, finance directly or indirectly, production processing storage and sale of poultry, poultry products poultry feed and equipment.
2. Provide services and assistance for the said purposes including capital, credit resource, technical and managerial.

Sikkim Hatchery Ltd.

1. Maintenance poultry breeder stock and production of commercial chips.
2. Supply/ marketing of chicks to the poultry farmers.
3. Supply of brooding equipments and poultry feed.

Sikkim Precision Industries Ltd.

1. Revenue generation.
2. Employment to socially backward class.

SITCO

1. To generate employment for socially backward classes and revenue.

Tea Board of Sikkim

1. Maintenance and operation of TEMI Tea Estate.

Government Fruit Preservation Factory

1. To encourage farmers to grow horticulture produce specially orange, passion fruit and dallae chilly.

Sikkim Tourism Ltd.

1. To run commercially government tourism facilities such as tourist lodges, hotels, restaurants and waysides amenities.
2. To market Sikkim Tourism.

Sikkim Handloom and Handicrafts Development Corp. Ltd

1. To provide marketing support to various individuals, craft persons, societies, co-operative organization and non-government organisations.
2. To train artisans and craft persons.

Khadi and Village Industries Board

1. Self-employment in rural areas to the promotion of Khadi and Village Industries.

State Trading Corp. Ltd.

1. To promote internal and external trade.
2. Attend to protocol duties of State Government at Kolkata and render assistance to the patients going to Kolkata for medical treatment.

The Denjong Agricultural Co-Operative Society Ltd., Agricultural Co-operative Society Ltd.

1. To promote and encourage spirit and practice of thrift self-help and co-operation among the members.

2. To provide marketing facilities for agricultural produce and animal husbandry products of its members within or outside the State.
3. To pool the agricultural produces of the members as well as non-members on such terms as may be settled between the parties and to collect, store sell the products of the members and providing shorting out, packing and transportation facilities for further marketings.
4. To enter into contract or agreement with any other agent departments of government, individual, association unions, corporation, company, co-operative societies, etc., for the purpose of trading or carrying on business of the society.
5. To supply agricultural goods on negotiated rate contract basis to army authorities.

Sikkim Consumer Co-operative Society

1. To supply stationeries, cookeries and sundry items to Government departments and retail consumers.
2. To cater the needs of general public and its shareholder by providing services with right things at price.
3. To check and balance the ever flexible market price.
4. To encourage thrift, self help and co-operation among the members of the society.

SIMFED

1. To arrange for the sale of agriculture product and other allied products of the members of the affiliated societies and other members to their best advantage.
2. To purchase and sale of Agricultural produce and the supply of agricultural inputs such as seed, fertilizer etc required by farmers.
3. To act as an agent of members societies for the disposal of produce.

4. To act on behalf of the State Government as an agent for receiving stocking and selling fertilizer dispatched on the state government account form the central pool.
5. To carry on trading in agricultural produce and other essential commodities as agent of the state government and distribution of controlled, non-controlled commodities procured from outside the state in suitable circumstances or behalf of the affiliated societies and other cooperatives.
6. To encourage general thrift, self-help and cooperation among the members—

Sikkim National Transport

1. To cater the transportation needs of the all government departments and central agencies such as Army, National Hydro Power Corporation, etc.
2. Provide transport services to public at large throughout the state.
3. Fulfil the social service requirement of providing transport on most of the routes having low occupancy and low population density.

Sikkim Power Development Corp.

1. To run small sized power projects.
2. To promote large sized power projects through IPPs.

State Energy and Department of Power

1. Provide power to domestic, commercial, agricultural and industrial sectors.
2. Provide power to public establishments and facilities.
3. Promote rural electrification.

SABCCO

1. Implement Center and State Government policies with regard to the welfare of the SCs, STs and OBCs living below Double Poverty Line.
2. Act as a State Channellising Agency for providing financial assistance to the target group from the Apex Corporations like National Schedule Finance Development Corp. Ltd, National Schedule Tribes Finance Development Corporation Ltd and National Backward Caste Finance Development Corporation Ltd at low interest rates.

Source: Interaction with the SLPEs Chiefs and Annexures 1.9 and 1.10.

ANNEXURE 1.5

RESOURCE MOBILIZATION BY SLPEs IN 2003-04

(Rs in Crore)

Name of the Enterprise	*State Equity*	*Other Equity*	*Total Equity*	*State Debt*	*Other Debt*	*Total Debt*	*Invest-ment*
SIDICO	10.7	6.36	17.04	2.03	0.59	2.62	19.66
State Bank of Sikkim	0.53	0.05	0.58	0	4.82	4.82	5.4
Sikkim State Co-operative Bank	9.49	0.51	10	0	0	0	9.36
Sikkim Jewels	5.62	0.78	6.4	0	0.56	0.56	7.05
Sikkim Hatchery	0.34	0.11	0.45	0	0	0	0.46
Sikkim Poultry	0	0	0	0	0	0	0
Sikkim Precision Industries	3.7	0	3.7	0	0	0	3.7
SITCO	11.2	0	11.22	0.52	0	0.52	11.74
Tea Board of Sikkim	22.71	0	22.71	0	0	0	22.71
Sikkim Milk Union	0.06	0	0.6	0.08	0	0.08	0.14
Govt. Fruit Preservation Factory	0	0	0	0	0	0	0
Sikkim Tourism	6.06	0	6.06	0	0	0	6.06
Sikkim Handloom and Handicrafts Dev. Corp. Ltd	0.80	0	0.80	0	0	0	0.80
Khadi and Village Board	0	0	0	0	0	0	12.01
State Trading Corp.	1.11	0	1.11	0	0	0	1.11
Sikkim Consumer Co-operative Soceity	0.17	0	0.17	0	0	0	0.17
SIMFED	0.94	0.08	1.02	0	0	0	1.02
Denjong	0.2	0	0.2	0	0	0	0.2
Sikkim National Transport Corp.	33.08	0	33.08	2.51	0	2.51	34.39
State Energy and Department of Power	514.79	0	514.79	0	0	0	514.79
Sikkim Power Development Corp.	53.01	0	53.01	0	0	0	53.01
SABCCO	8.04	1.51	9.55	8.21	3.74	11.95	21.50

0 – No mobilization from the source.

Source: Annexure 1.9.

ANNEXURE 1.6

PROFIT PERFORMANCE OF SLPEs IN 2003-04

Name of the Enterprise	*Net profit (Rs. in crore)*	*Investment (Rs. in crore)*	*Net profit on Total Investment (in %)*
SIDICO	0.46	19.66	2.34
State Bank of Sikkim	–0.95	5.4	–17.59
Sikkim State Co-operative Bank	0.69	9.36	7.37
Sikkim Jewels	–0.38	7.04	–5.40
Sikkim Hatchery	0	0.46	0.00
Sikkim Poultry	–0.08	0.79	–10.13
Sikkim Precision Industries	0.04	3.7	1.08
SITCO	–3.29	11.74	–28.02
Tea Board of Sikkim	0.03	22.71	0.13
Sikkim Milk Union	–1.03	0.14	–735.71
Govt. Fruit Preservation Factory	0.02	0	0.00
Sikkim Tourism	–0.64	6.06	–10.56
Sikkim Handloom and Handicrafts Dev. Corp. Ltd.	0	0.8	0.00
Khadi and Village Board	0	12.01	0.00
State Trading Corp.	0.66	1.11	59.46
Sikkim Consumer Co-operative Soceity	0.008	0.17	4.71
SIMFED	0.19	1.02	18.63
Denjong	–0.46	0.2	–230.00
Sikkim Nationalised Transport Corp.	–4.2	34.39	–12.21
State Energy and Department of Power	–22.69	514.79	0.00
Sikkim Power Dev. Corp.	0	53.01	0.00
SABCCO	–1.12	21.5	–5.21
Total	–32.74	726.06	–4.51

0 – Not available.

Source: Annexure 1.9.

ANNEXURE 1.7

CHARACTERISTICS OF SLPEs IN THE STATE OF SIKKIM

Name of SLPE and Year of establishment	*Form of Organisation*	*Market Structure (MS) and Activities (A)*	*Financial Status and Physical performance*	*Employees*	*Social purpose*	*Financial System & management and interface with Government*	*Performance improvement plan*	*SWOT Analysis*	*Problems encountered*	*Strategic initiatives*
Sikkim Jewels Ltd (SJL) (7/2/1972)	Govt. Company	MS: Competitive A: Watch Jewels, Industrial Jewels Berings, rotor magents, and disposable syrenges	A company incurring marginal losses	125 Mgl 20 Nmgl 105	Providing employment to local	Budgeting and internal audit exist in the company	Wage Bill reduction from Rs. 10.5 lakhs per month to Rs. 6.5 lakhs per month	S: Good past record, new markets for health products and micro precision instruments	5% Export incentives not given amounting Rs. 0.25 crore due to non-implementation of Central ITAct	New investments planned
			Physical performance: Capacity utilisation is 100 per cent			Government directed pricing	Setting up disposable syringes and needles project to counter decline in demand of industrial jewels	W: declining domestic demand, Obsolete machinery	GoS has to pay Rs. 0.40 crore towards VRS	Diversification of product line

(*Contd.*)

ANNEXURE 1.7: (Contd.)

Name of SLPE and Year of establishment	*Form of Organisation*	*Market Structure (MS) and Activities (A)*	*Financial Status and Physical performance*	*Employees*	*Social purpose*	*Financial System & management and interface with Government*	*Performance improvement plan*	*SWOT Analysis*	*Problems encountered*	*Strategic initiatives*
						No delegation and decentral-ization	Enhancing capacity to 10 millions costing Rs 2.50 crore on import of machinery	O: Excessive staff		Global linkages for marketing
						Manpower planning and performance appraisal systems exists	To set up rotor magnets for quartz watches for exports worth Rs. 7.00 crore	T: low priority assigned by the government and global competition		
						Performance evaluation methods non-existence	Proposes to spend Rs. 0.50 crore on technical travel and training			
						Government nominees dominate the Board	Proposes to produce tiny jewels in micron tolerance			

(Contd.)

ANNEXURE 1.7: (Contd.)

Name of SLPE and Year of establishment	Form of Organisation	Market Structure (MS) and Activities (A)	Financial Status and Physical performance	Employees	Social purpose	Financial System & management and interface with Government	Performance improvement plan	SWOT Analysis	Problems encountered	Strategic initiatives
						Tenure of the Board of Directors not specified	Proposes to produce high value iow volume defense products			
						No R&D	Proposes to modernize plant by inducting latest state of art technology costing Rs. 0.30 crore.			
						Interaction with government: low	VRS given to 91 employees			
Sikkim Tourism Dev. Corp. Ltd (21/09/98)	Govt. Company	MS: Competitive A: Tourism Services, transport (helicopter service) and market	Financial Status: 100 per cent state government equity, no long term debt, loss making, errioson of	89 MGI 4 NM 85	Employment to 85 persons, ^apacity building for tourism and village tourism	No costing systems and standard costing, management reporting systems non existence, Govt.	Occupancy rate of hotels is planned to be improved	S: Tourist traffic is increasing, pro-government policies for tourism, properties	Non-managerial employees are too high in numbers, Board meets seldom, Helicopter service is affected by non-	Post of GM abolished and organization is being made lien

(Contd.)

ANNEXURE 1.7: (Contd.)

Name of SLPE and Year of establishment	*Form of Organisation*	*Market Structure (MS) and Activities (A)*	*Financial Status and Physical performance*	*Employees*	*Social purpose*	*Financial System & management and interface with Government*	*Performance improvement plan*	*SWOT Analysis*	*Problems encountered*	*Strategic initiatives*
		consultancy to tourism department	networth, accumulated losses, scanty contribution, negative operating profits, advertisement expenses is 1% of total revenue			nominees dominate the board, partial deligation, non-pricing systems, no costing system, no manpower planning, and no R&D		require vast repairs	availability of spare parts, Not connected by internet, Untrained middle and low management	
			Physical performance: Average occupancy rate			The company has vision to develop new tourist destination, construct and manage new hotels and provide facilities for tourism and tourists		W: Low share capital base, Transfer of departmental personnel has promoted unhealthy culture		Some key properties have been privatised such as Hotel Mayur, Singhik, Tsongo, and Alpine Cafateria
						Internal audit and budgeting systems partly exists		O: The state has become a popular tourist destination,		VRS to excess staff is being considered

(Contd.)

ANNEXURE 1.7: (Contd.)

Name of SLPE and Year of establishment	*Form of Organisation*	*Market Structure (MS) and Activities (A)*	*Financial Status and Physical performance*	*Employees*	*Social purpose*	*Financial System & management and interface with Government*	*Performance improvement plan*	*SWOT Analysis*	*Problems encountered*	*Strategic initiatives*
								Investors have shown keen interest in taking out properties of the company		
						Interface with the government: Very frequent interaction with Minister and political chairperson, The political chairperson instructs on pricing, investment, personnel selection, purchase of inputs and day-to-day decisions		T: Natural disasters are a great threat, any agitation in WB could upset the apple cart		To bridge the resource gap the corpo-ration is pressing upon the govern-ment to handover Northhil Hotel, which is currently under the contoll of tourism department

(Contd.)

ANNEXURE 1.7: (Contd.)

Name of SLPE and Year of establishment	*Form of Organisation*	*Market Structure (MS) and Activities (A)*	*Financial Status and Physical performance*	*Employees*	*Social purpose*	*Financial System & management and interface with Government*	*Performance improvement plan*	*SWOT Analysis*	*Problems encountered*	*Strategic initiatives*
Manufacturing										
Tea Board of Sikkim (1/6/1974)	Departmental Enterprise	MS: Competitive A: Black Tea (Orthodox)	Continious loss making enterprise, Stagnent capital employed, receeding net worth, sacanty contribution and negative operating profit	455 Magl -10 NM 444	Use of local resources and employment to locals	Being a departmental enterprise, no corporate systems exists	Non	S: Temi Tea has good demand and highly competitive market	Excessive staff, expansion not possible	
			Physical performance: 100% capacity utilisation			Interaction with govt.: Very low		O: Brand building opportunities exits	Latest technology for processing not available	
								T: Receding demand of tea	Expansion not possible	
									Plantation is getting aged	

(Contd.)

ANNEXURE 1.7: (Contd.)

Name of SLPE and Year of establishment	Form of Organisation	Market Structure (MS) and Activities (A)	Financial Status and Physical performance	Employees	Social purpose	Financial System & management and interface with Government	Performance improvement plan	SWOT Analysis	Problems encountered	Strategic initiatives
The Denjong Agricultural Co-operative Society Ltd (08/02/65)	Co-operative society	MS: Competitive A: Supply of fruits, vegetables and meat products	Continuously profit making company, cent percent government equity, debt free, Positive working capital, Increasing networth, High turnover, High contingent liability and High unsettled liabilities	112 Mgl 2 NM 60 Casual 40		Government officials dominated Board, Empowered board and chief executive, Budgeting, internal audit and pricing systems exist, MIS systems non existence, R&D non-existant, Manpower planning does not exist, Board meets four times a year, and Board and CEO decide upon hiring and retrenchment	Moderni-sation	S: High turnover,	Dependence on army for supplies on negotiabted contract rates	Rationalisation of manpower under VRS

(Contd.)

ANNEXURE 1.7: (Contd.)

Name of SLPE and Year of establishment	Form of Organisation	Market Structure (MS) and Activities (A)	Financial Status and Physical performance	Employees	Social purpose	Financial System & management and interface with Government	Performance improvement plan	SWOT Analysis	Problems encountered	Strategic initiatives
						Interface with government: Low	Rationalisation of labour force	W: high overhead expenses		Setting up of markets in retails/ wholesale chain outlets
								O: Expansion and diversification of business such as cold storage, chain outlets, agro processing and flour mills.		Increase in share capital
								T: Competitive market and over staffing		Modernisation of flour mills

(Contd.)

ANNEXURE 1.7: (Contd.)

Name of SLPE and Year of establishment	Form of Organisation	Market Structure (MS) and Activities (A)	Financial Status and Physical performance	Manpower	Social purpose	Financial System & management and interface with Government	Performance improvement plan	SWOT Analysis	Problems encountered	Strategic initiatives	Restructuring
SABCCO (1996)		MS: Monopoly A: Financing SC, ST and OBCs through margin money schemes, Mahila Samridhi Yogana, SLGs.	Continiously loss making, Increase in net worth due to equity infusion, Excessive direct cost, Negative working capital, High interest burden, Revenue subsidy and Guarantees from State Govt.	16 Mgl. 4 NM -12	Promote activities related to women through specific schemes	FS: Absence of costing, R&D and pricing systems, MIS systems non-existence, Govt. officials dominated by the board and Empowered executives	Micro Credit Finance to be introduced	S: Provides financial assistance to the weakest section of the society and covers the entire rural population of the state	Recovery of loans faces a major problem as the target group belongs to people leaving below poverty line	Loans on cheaper interest rates as compared to Banks	Financial restructuring: Timely release of share capital, need for grant in aid for meeting administrative costs, release of replace-ment of repayment schedules of old loans
					Promoting SHGs	Interface with Government: Adequate	Tourism related schemes	W: Lack of professional manpower, Lack of proper recruitment policies, Lack	Delayed release of share capital	Undertaking financial restructuring	Manpower restructuring: free and fare hand in recruitment of professionals

(Contd.)

ANNEXURE 1.7: (Contd.)

Name of SLPE and Year of establishment	*Form of Organisation*	*Market Structure (MS) and Activities (A)*	*Financial Status and Physical performance*	*Manpower*	*Social purpose*	*Financial System & management and interface with Government*	*Performance improvement plan*	*SWOT Analysis*	*Problems encountered*	*Strategic initiatives*	*Restructuring*
								of Govt. support for share capital and grant in aid, Failure to recover 100 per cent dues			
							Educational loan schemes	O: Total financial dependence on the state, Only medium to further GoS policies with regard to social welfare	Grant-in-aid towards meeting administrative costs not released	Proposes to recruit professionals	Organi-sational restructuring: induction of professionals to boast performance
								T: disconti-nuation of the Central and the State Govt. support and tough competitions from banks	Aged loans and revenue subsidy of 0.16 crores	Recovery of loans from deneficiaries by holding default recovery camps, filling cases under	

(Contd.)

ANNEXURE 1.7: (Contd.)

Name of SLPE and Year of establishment	*Form of Organisation*	*Market Structure (MS) and Activities (A)*	*Financial Status and Physical performance*	*Manpower*	*Social purpose*	*Financial System & management and interface with Government*	*Performance improvement plan*	*SWOT Analysis*	*Problems encountered*	*Strategic initiatives*	*Restructuring*
								on account of low interest rate, easier availabilty of loans, simplified documentation process		lok adalat and SPDR Act. The company proposes to involve local MLA's and Panchanyats in the recovery of debts	
									Inadequate qualified persons and lack of funds for management development programmes	Seek help to: liquidate and writeoff bad and douobtful debts, extend VRS, develop a new loans and train officers and staff	

(Contd.)

ANNEXURE 1.7: (Contd.)

Name of SLPE and Year of establishment	*Form of Organisation*	*Market Structure (MS) and Activities (A)*	*Financial Status and Physical performance*	*Employees*	*Social purpose*	*Financial System & management and interface with Government*	*Performance improvement plan*	*SWOT Analysis*	*Problems encountered*	*Strategic initiatives*
Sikkim Precision Industries Ltd (1999)	Govt. Company	MS: Completely dependent on Principal, Bharat Electronics Ltd. Competitive A: Manufacturing semi-conductor devices	Profit making,	60 Mgl 4, Nm50 casual 6	Employment to 50 persons including handicapped	Absence of budget, internal audit, costing, pricing and MIS	Exploring international markets	S: Skilled manpower	Completely dependent on BEL Ltd	Restructuring (product, market and technological) is planned costing Rs. 90 lakhs
			Physical performance: 50 per cent capacity utilised		Promote industry culture	Interface with Government: Very low		W: No labour unrest	Low Capacity utilisation	40 employess will be recruited due to restructuring costing to Rs. 1.2 Lakh per month
								O: Non-pollutant enterprise, Good scope for diversifying activities	Low innovation	The company proposes to set up to-92 assembly plant within the same premises will will generate

(Contd.)

ANNEXURE 1.7: (Contd.)

Name of SLPE and Year of establishment	Form of Organisation	Market Structure (MS) and Activities (A)	Financial Status and Physical performance	Employees	Social purpose	Financial System & management and interface with Government	Performance improvement plan	SWOT Analysis	Problems encountered	Strategic initiatives
										employment for 40 persons
								T: Fully dependent on Bharat Electronics Ltd, Logistics problems, Competition from chinese devices and Mother-child relationship could cause problems	Low turnover	
Sikkim Handloom and Handicrafts Development Corporation Ltd (16-10-2001)	Sikkim Handloom and Handicrafts Dev. Corp. Ltd	MS: Competitive A: marketing of handicrafts items such as carpets, choktse, Thanka, Handloom and multicasts	Loss making and Dependence on external institutes for working capital	13 Mgl 1. Nmg 12	Uplift the socio-economic status	Non-existence and Very low degree of professionalism	Setting up a of pilot project to establish nine handicraft societies	S: Favourable government policy	High dependence on the department	setting up of marketing chain through out Sikkim

(Contd.)

ANNEXURE 1.7: (Contd.)

Name of SLPE and Year of establishment	*Form of Organisation*	*Market Structure (MS) and Activities (A)*	*Financial Status and Physical performance*	*Employees*	*Social purpose*	*Financial System & management and interface with Government*	*Performance improvement plan*	*SWOT Analysis*	*Problems encountered*	*Strategic initiatives*
			Physical performance: Low turnover			Interface with Govt. Satisfactory		W: No grants in aid	Very short tenure for chief executives	Enhancing share capital
								O: Good market T: Taxes	Inexperienced personnel	Setting up a desing centre with modern technology
Sikkim Poultry Development Corp Ltd (1991)	Govt. Company	MS: Competitive A: Trading in Poultry feed, equipments and products	Continiously loss making, Unable to fund working capital and no money for capital expenditure	6 Magl. 1 Casual 5	Increase the income of grass root farmers through poutlry farming	Budgeting, internal audit, costing and pricing systems are extnsion of the government systems		S: A government company	Managerially very weak	A consultant has been appointed to suggest a study plan
						Interface with Government: Very low		W: No enterprise element	Lacks enterprise orientation	
								O: Huge demand	Finances are in shambles	
								T: Competition form private sector poultries		

(Contd.)

ANNEXURE 1.7: (Contd.)

Name of SLPE and Year of establishment	*Form of Organisation*	*Market Structure (MS) and Activities (A)*	*Financial Status and Physical performance*	*Employees*	*Social purpose*	*Financial System & management and interface with Government*	*Performance improvement plan*	*SWOT Analysis*	*Problems encountered*	*Strategic initiatives*
Sikkim Hatchery Ltd (1994)	Government Company with private sector participation (Sri Venkateshwara Hatcheries	MS: Competitive A: Poultry breeders, Produces commercial chicks, Supply/marketing of chicks and Supply of Poultry feed	Loss making, Dearth of working capital, Networth erosion, and Contingent liabilities	15 Mg 1, Nml 2, Casual 15	To increase the imcome of grass root people/ famers through poultry farming	Budgeting, internal audit, costing and pricing systems are extnsion of the government systems	A consultant has been appointed to prepare a turnover project	S: A government company		Working capital is being sought from financial institution/ government
						Interface with Government: Very low		W: No enterprise element		
								O: Huge demand		
								T: Competition form private sector poultries		
			case by SBI in debt recovery tribunal of Rs. 0.40 crores							

(Contd.)

ANNEXURE 1.7: (Contd.)

Name of SLPE and Year of establishment	Form of Organisation	Market Structure (MS) and Activities (A)	Financial Status and Physical performance	Employees	Social purpose	Financial System & management and interface with Government	Performance improvement plan	SWOT Analysis	Problems encountered	Strategic initiatives
SITCO (1976)	Govt. Company	MS: Competitive A: Digital and Analog Watches and TV Speakers	Loss making company, negative contribution, high administrative and interest costs, decline in capital employed, and negative reserves and surpluses	146 Mag. 22 Nmgl 87 Casual 37	Employment generation: has given employment to 1000 people since inception (90 per cent are women)	Rudimentary budget, and internal audit, Cost management is non-existant, Satisfactory middle management, Govt. dominated Board and Part-time Directors representing professionals are nominal in numbers	115 employees have availed of VRS costing Rs 272 lakhs	S: 28 year old company having core competency in homology and electronics field, Association with industrial gaints like HMT, BEL, BPL, skilled manpower, good industrial environment, one of the few watch companies enlisted with the CSD of the Defence Ministry for the supply of watches and Availability of ample	Timely release of share capital from Gos	Rs 2 crore spent on additional machinery

(Contd.)

ANNEXURE 1.7: (Contd.)

Name of SLPE and Year of establishment	*Form of Organisation*	*Market Structure (MS) and Activities (A)*	*Financial Status and Physical performance*	*Employees*	*Social purpose*	*Financial System & management and interface with Government*	*Performance improvement plan*	*SWOT Analysis*	*Problems encountered*	*Strategic initiatives*
								infrastructure, buildings, space		
			Physical performance: 30 per cent capacity utilised		National integration	Interface with Government: Very low	Brand promotion	W: Locational disadvantage, Limited brand awareness of products and No R&D	Sundry Debtors of 2.5 crores to be writtenoff	Restructuing to add to the wage bill to Rs 30 Lakhs per annum as 15 new jobs will be created.
					Promote industrial culture		Channel management	O: Workers require further training and skill enhancement and Climatic conditions suitable for electronics, IT, watch and other precision industries	Shortage of working capital to supply speaker to BPL/ Onida and to increase th production of speakers	Increase in market share through CSD and direct marketing

(Contd.)

ANNEXURE 1.7: (Contd.)

Name of SLPE and Year of establishment	Form of Organisation	Market Structure (MS) and Activities (A)	Financial Status and Physical performance	Employees	Social purpose	Financial System & management and interface with Government	Performance improvement plan	SWOT Analysis	Problems encountered	Strategic initiatives
								T: Competition from organised, unorganies and overseas competition		VRS to about 40 employees estimated to cost Rs 1.50 crore
										Activity restructuring: launching of higher variants and models of watches, time pieces and clocks, enlargement of product profile management system
										Induction and training of required manpower in design and development area of speakers and watches

(Contd.)

ANNEXURE 1.7: (Contd.)

Name of SLPE and Year of establishment	*Form of Organisation*	*Market Structure (MS) and Activities (A)*	*Financial Status and Physical performance*	*Employees*	*Social purpose*	*Financial System & management and interface with Government*	*Performance improvement plan*	*SWOT Analysis*	*Problems encountered*	*Strategic initiatives*
										Manpower restructuring: Training of manpower on shop floor, giving VRS to around 40 excess employees
										Technological Restructuring: Setting up of desing and development wing for speakers and sourcing of approproate required technology
										Financial Restructuring: Release of share capital toward

(*Contd.*)

ANNEXURE 1.7: (Contd.)

Name of SLPE and Year of establishment	Form of Organisation	Market Structure (MS) and Activities (A)	Financial Status and Physical performance	Employees	Social purpose	Financial System & management and interface with Government	Performance improvement plan	SWOT Analysis	Problems encountered	Strategic initiatives
										product/ activity restructuring and repayment of bank loans and write-off bad debts
Government Fruit Preservation Factory (1965)	Govt. Company	MS: Competitive A: Produces Squashes, Juices, Jams, Pickles, Sauces and Tinned Fruits	Decline in working capital, Profit earning company, and Instable sales	60 Mgr 3, Nml 6,Casual 3	Distribution of Seeds and seedlings to local farmer, Providing training to locals to make pickels and jams and to provide training to farmers in farming baby corn, dallae chilles etc	Budgeting, MIS and pricing are non-existant	The factory is running on adhoc basis	S: Brand Sikkim Supreme is the major strength	Exemption from sales tax and income tax not given	GoS may either accept turnover plan by GoI or Privatise / going for closure

(Contd.)

ANNEXURE 1.7: (Contd.)

Name of SLPE and Year of establishment	Form of Organisation	Market Structure (MS) and Activities (A)	Financial Status and Physical performance	Employees	Social purpose	Financial System & management and interface with Government	Performance improvement plan	SWOT Analysis	Problems encountered	Strategic initiatives
		New products added includes babycorn, sweet corn, dallae chilly in veniger	Physical performance: 15 per cent capacity utilized			Interface with Government: Poor		W: Lack of continuity of policy	No purchase preference by the government	
								O: Lower customers and market penitration	Promised budgetory support not extended	
								T: Competition and inadequate market development and promotion	Turnaround plan approved by Govt. of India on matching basis not honoured by GoS	

(Contd.)

ANNEXURE 1.7: (Contd.)

Name of SLPE and Year of establishment	*Form of Organisation*	*Market Structure (MS) and Activities (A)*	*Financial Status and Physical performance*	*Employees*	*Social purpose*	*Financial System & management and interface with Government*	*Performance improvement plan*	*SWOT Analysis*	*Problems encountered*	*Strategic initiatives*
SIDICO (1977)	Govt. Company	MS: Monopoly A: Financing small, medium and large units	Declining accumulated losses, Currently profit making and Declared dividends in 1996-97 and 2001-02	34 Mg 19, Nml 15	Industrial promotion and employment generation through assisted units	Cost management non-existant, weak internal audit, Poor monitoring of assisted units, Weak project appraisal system, decision-making power vests with government, No manpower planning and no manpower training and development	Setting up guidline/ counselling cell	S: The only development financial institution. No default in repayment of re-finance., Track record of profit making from the last five years, High rate of interest	Lack of viable proposals	Debt Free company
						Interface with the Government: Moderate	Improving recoveries	W: Decline in equity support from Govt., high administrative cost	Investment in assisted units of Rs 2.58 crore in equity, generation WEBCOM not generation any returns	Promoting new generation industries such as Software Park

(*Contd.*)

ANNEXURE 1.7: (Contd.)

Name of SLPE and Year of establishment	*Form of Organisation*	*Market Structure (MS) and Activities (A)*	*Financial Status and Physical performance*	*Employees*	*Social purpose*	*Financial System & management and interface with Government*	*Performance improvement plan*	*SWOT Analysis*	*Problems encountered*	*Strategic initiatives*
								O: Rapid, economic and industrial development of the state	large number of sutis field under SPDRA are pending	extending State Financial Act S.29,30 and 31
								T: Competetion with commercial banks	High administrative costs	Extending coverage to ianncia, housing, poultry, piggery and diary sectors
									Discontinuation of disbursement of central subsidies	Involvement in infrastructure development
									Competition from NEDFC and SABCCO	Enhancing HRD compentcies

(Contd.)

ANNEXURE 1.7: (Contd.)

Name of SLPE and Year of establishment	*Form of Organisation*	*Market Structure (MS) and Activities (A)*	*Financial Status and Physical performance*	*Employees*	*Social purpose*	*Financial System & management and interface with Government*	*Performance improvement plan*	*SWOT Analysis*	*Problems encountered*	*Strategic initiatives*
State Bank of Sikkim (1968)	Public Corporation	MS: Non-competitive A: Commercial lending, investment and treasury functions	Currently profit making	271 MG 50, NML 221		Rs 6.81 crore loans are being shown due in the name of deceased borrowers	27 employees availing of VRS costing Rs 82 lakhs of which Rs 80 lakhs given by GoS	Own charter Bankers to GoS	Tough competition from commercial banks	Sound corporate vision of striving and achieving premier position as a superier financial institution
			Physical performance: High advances, major part of equity contribution from GoS, Good leverage, Huge losses on account of Interest waver scheme amounting to			Outstanding of loan of Rs 2.05 crore in the name of officers and staff of SBS. Rs. 36.03 lakhs is outstanding against 1 expired employees		Better understanding of the local economy	High administrative costs	Concentration on other income

(Contd.)

ANNEXURE 1.7: (Contd.)

Name of SLPE and Year of establishment	Form of Organisation	Market Structure (MS) and Activities (A)	Financial Status and Physical performance	Employees	Social purpose	Financial System & management and interface with Government	Performance improvement plan	SWOT Analysis	Problems encountered	Strategic initiatives
			Rs. 25 crore, Increasing trend in business, Positive contribution and gross margin and low Capital adequacy							
						Poor securtiy systems leading to non-recovery of loans of Rs 4 crore under SPDRA		Lack of adequate equity	Poor services offered by non-trained staff	New schemes such as loans to Govt. employees without any collateral upto Rs 10 lakhs
						Only Rs 2 lakh spent on advertisement during 2003-04		Untrained manpower	No networking	Triming the employees strength. 70-80 persons could be provided VRS subject to appointment of 20 qualified persons.

(Contd.)

ANNEXURE 1.7: (Contd.)

Name of SLPE and Year of establishment	*Form of Organisation*	*Market Structure (MS) and Activities (A)*	*Financial Status and Physical performance*	*Employees*	*Social purpose*	*Financial System & management and interface with Government*	*Performance improvement plan*	*SWOT Analysis*	*Problems encountered*	*Strategic initiatives*
						Financial and administrative powers deligated upto the power of GMs'		Non-computerisation	Very poor equity base of Rs 0.58 lakhs against the minimum expected of Rs 30 crores	VRS cost Rs. 5 to 6 crores @ Rs 7 lakh per employee
						Interface with government: good interaction		Competetion from other commercial banks	No monitoring	
State Trading Corp. (1972)	Public Corporation	MS: Competitive A: Supply of all types of materials required by Govt. departments	Debt Free, Sound Reserves, Profit making, accumulated profits, and Positive networth	108, ML8 NML 70 casual 27	Protocol duties of State Govt. at Kolkatta, renders assistance to Sikkimies patentis at Kolkata	Internal Audit, Pricing and MIS exists in rudimentary form, MIS, Budgeting does not exist, Government nominees dominate the Board, Dividend paying company	Improving communication with Govt. departments	S: Procurement backup in terms of public corporation	Competition from private suppliers	Closure of Kolkata and Siliguri branches

(Contd.)

ANNEXURE 1.7: (Contd.)

Name of SLPE and Year of establishment	*Form of Organisation*	*Market Structure (MS) and Activities (A)*	*Financial Status and Physical performance*	*Employees*	*Social purpose*	*Financial System & management and interface with Government*	*Performance improvement plan*	*SWOT Analysis*	*Problems encountered*	*Strategic initiatives*
						Interface with government: Low	Controlling administrative expenses to work within margins offered by suppliers	W: Non-cooperation of Govt. departments	Govt. departments prefer to place direct orders on suppliers	Encouraging surplus employees to take VRS
							Better stock keeping	O: Burgeoning demand for supplies	Non-payment by Govt. department	Fostering transparency in procurement of proprietary and non - proprietary items
								T: Response time to fulfil the demand and payments from Govt. departments	Lack of sensitisation about supply chain management	

(Contd.)

ANNEXURE 1.7: (Contd.)

Name of SLPE and Year of establishment	*Form of Organisation*	*Market Structure (MS) and Activities (A)*	*Financial Status and Physical performance*	*Employees*	*Social purpose*	*Financial System & management and interface with Government*	*Performance improvement plan*	*SWOT Analysis*	*Problems encountered*	*Strategic initiatives*
Khadi and Village Industries Board (1978)	Public Corporation	MS: competitive A: Engaged in production and sale of khadi and village industry products	Loss making, decline in turnover, high direct costs	83 Mg 14, NML 65 Part-time 100	Provides self-employment in rural area	Govt nomiees led Board, no budgeting, pricing, costing and internal audit systems, no training for employees and no R&D	Proposes to offer VRS 40 more persons costing Rs 1.60 crores	S: Old legacy from Chogyal days	Dearth of money for expenditure, poor advertisement, Un-remunerative prices to weavers, spinners and rural artisan, and no money to pay gratuity to retired people	VRS to 16 employees Rs 0.65 crore
			Physical performance: 20 % capacity used			Interface with government: low		W: Completely dependent on government, large unemployed rural masses and young fork not taking to *Charka* and village industries		New sales outlets, and proposes to use other channels of sales

(Contd.)

ANNEXURE 1.7: (Contd.)

Name of SLPE and Year of establishment	*Form of Organisation*	*Market Structure (MS) and Activities (A)*	*Financial Status and Physical performance*	*Employees*	*Social purpose*	*Financial System & management and interface with Government*	*Performance improvement plan*	*SWOT Analysis*	*Problems encountered*	*Strategic initiatives*
										Technology upgradation for *Charka* and *Kargha* costing Rs 0.12 crore
										Model employership will cost Rs 1.06 crore on CPF, VRS, pension, repairs and renovations
										EDPs for borrowers under margin money scheme from banks
										Efforts for financial assistance from KVIC for borrowers

(*Contd.*)

ANNEXURE 1.7: (Contd.)

Name of SLPE and Year of establishment	*Form of Organisation*	*Market Structure (MS) and Activities (A)*	*Financial Status and Physical performance*	*Employees*	*Social purpose*	*Financial System & management and interface with Government*	*Performance improvement plan*	*SWOT Analysis*	*Problems encountered*	*Strategic initiatives*
Sikkim Consumer Co-operative society (1975)	Co-operative Society	MS: Competitive A: supply of stationeries, cookeries and sundry items	Profit making	27 Mg 2,Nml 22, Causal 3	To provide right services at right time	A tentative budget is prepared every year and internal audit is prepared every year	None	Purchase preference for consumer goods	Competition with STC, SIMFED, Denjong Co-operative Society.	Trying to become whole sale agent of several companies
					To act as a countervailing force on price fund	No costing and MIS systems	Conversion into a federation to act as a whole sale agency for controlled and non-controlled agencies	Outstanding of government departments of Rs 1.19 crore	Inadequate working capital	
						Government dominated Boards		Conversion into a federation to act as a whole sale agency for controlled and non-controlled agencies	Requirement of office premises -	

(Contd.)

ANNEXURE 1.7: (Contd.)

Name of SLPE and Year of establishment	Form of Organisation	Market Structure (MS) and Activities (A)	Financial Status and Physical performance	Employees	Social purpose	Financial System & management and interface with Government	Performance improvement plan	SWOT Analysis	Problems encountered	Strategic initiatives
						Interface with government: moderate		Dependence on government for sales		
Sikkim Co-operative Bank (1975)	Co-operative Society	MS: Non-Competitive A: Serve as an Apex organization of co-operative societies, raise deposits from members and to do business as per Section 5 and 6(1) of BRA 1949			Help the farmers in agricultural operations	Internal audit, Budgeting systems exits but in a rudimentary form, Pricing and MIS systems do not exists and Lack of computerization	Greater reliance on Crop Insurance			Networking with NABARD for disbursements under non-firm sector
					Balance agricultural development in the four districts	Interface with government: Satisfactory				Developing 10 MPCS under piolt project from NABARD and MPCS
										Good recovery system

(Contd.)

ANNEXURE 1.7: (Contd.)

Name of SLPE and Year of establishment	*Form of Organisation*	*Market Structure (MS) and Activities (A)*	*Financial Status and Physical performance*	*Employees*	*Social purpose*	*Financial System & management and interface with Government*	*Performance improvement plan*	*SWOT Analysis*	*Problems encountered*	*Strategic initiatives*
SIMFED	Co-operative Society	MS: Competitive A: Trade and Service			Ensuring price support to cash crop farmers	Budgeting, costing, pricing and internal audit systems are ineffective		Deals with cash crops, confined to marketing of cash crops, processing units for cash crops, and poor infrastructure and systems	Poor working capital base,	Diversification through: Ginger and cardamom processing plants, corporative tourism, co-operative manufacturing unit and becoming C&F of agent for manufacturers
						Computeri-sation of accounts of purchase and sales doe not exists			Inadequate infrastructure, stock in trade and marketing skills	Conducts open auctions for cadmium
						Interface with Govt.: low			Failure as price leader	Auctions in different districts

(Contd.)

ANNEXURE 1.7: (Contd.)

Name of SLPE and Year of establishment	*Form of Organisation*	*Market Structure (MS) and Activities (A)*	*Financial Status and Physical performance*	*Employees*	*Social purpose*	*Financial System & management and interface with Government*	*Performance improvement plan*	*SWOT Analysis*	*Problems encountered*	*Strategic initiatives*
									Ban on usage of chemical fertilizer	Marketing intelligence for developing comprehen-sive plans
										One time government grant of Rs 10 crore towards working capital
										Allotment of land from government towards infrastructure development
										Computeri-sation at the cost of Rs 2 crore to be granted by the government

(*Contd.*)

ANNEXURE 1.7: (Contd.)

Name of SLPE and Year of establishment	*Form of Organisation*	*Market Structure (MS) and Activities (A)*	*Financial Status and Physical performance*	*Employees*	*Social purpose*	*Financial System & management and interface with Government*	*Performance improvement plan*	*SWOT Analysis*	*Problems encountered*	*Strategic initiatives*
Sikkim National Transport (1944)	Departmental Enterprise	MS: competitive A: Fulfil transportation needs of all government departments, central agencies, army and rural and urban masses through the fleet of trucks and buses	Continuously loss making, negative internal resource generation, negative plan contributions, and declining earning per bus km	957 Mg57, Nml 900	To fulfill the transport needs of army and rural and urban masses	Being an extension of govt. department, no autonomous financial and management systems, ineffective pricing systems, and imbalance fare structure,		Long experiencod department	Increase in bus staff ratio of 1:9.2	GoS is contemplating to bring down the age of the fleet and also enlarge it
			Physical performance: 45% occupancy ratio			Customer relationship management non existant		Appendage of GoS suffering from Govt. systems and procedures	Low staff productivity of 16.26 km per day per worker	GoS is contemplating to introduce VRS to reduce unwarranted staff

(*Contd.*)

ANNEXURE 1.7: (Contd.)

Name of SLPE and Year of establishment	Form of Organisation	Market Structure (MS) and Activities (A)	Financial Status and Physical performance	Employees	Social purpose	Financial System & management and interface with Government	Performance improvement plan	SWOT Analysis	Problems encountered	Strategic initiatives
						Interface with government: moderate		Incapacity to serve the increasing transportation needs in a customer friendly manner	Declining fuel efficiency of 3.05 km per liter	
									Age profile of buses and trucks is highly unfavorable as 106 buses out of 192 on march 31, 2003 were 10 + years old	
									Concessional/ free travel facilities as directed by GoS	

(Contd.)

ANNEXURE 1.7: (Contd.)

Name of SLPE and Year of establishment	*Form of Organisation*	*Market Structure (MS) and Activities (A)*	*Financial Status and Physical performance*	*Employees*	*Social purpose*	*Financial System & management and interface with Government*	*Performance improvement plan*	*SWOT Analysis*	*Problems encountered*	*Strategic initiatives*
State Energy and Department of Power (1967)	Departmental Enterprise	MS: Non-competitive A: Provide power to domestic, commercial, agricultural and industrial sectors, Provide power to public establish-ments and facilities and promote rural electrification	Continuously heavy loss making, negative internal resource generation, declining earning per bus km and price-cost relationship	2717 Mg 100, Nml 2617	Power to rural areas, agriculturists and industrial units	25 % capacity utilisation and load factor 40 %	Focusing on project management	Tremendous potential of growth and engine for development	High T&D losses and low tariff	Reduction of T& D losses from 52 % to 38 % by 2006 -07, 15 % by 2011-12
						Interface with government: very high			Highly overstaffed on the administrative side but understaffed on the technical side	Increase in tariff to cover costs

(Contd.)

ANNEXURE 1.7: (Contd.)

Name of SLPE and Year of establishment	Form of Organisation	Market Structure (MS) and Activities (A)	Financial Status and Physical performance	Employees	Social purpose	Financial System & management and interface with Government	Performance improvement plan	SWOT Analysis	Problems encountered	Strategic initiatives
									Conflict between the role of department and the State Power Devel. Corporation	Reorganization through SBIs for generation, transmission and distribution
										corporatisation to setup 3 companies
										Promoting IPPs in power generation through BOAT/ BOOT/ DBOAT
										Setting up of an independent Tariff Regulatory Authority

(Contd.)

ANNEXURE 1.7: (Contd.)

Name of SLPE and Year of establishment	Form of Organisation	Market Structure (MS) and Activities (A)	Financial Status and Physical performance	Employees	Social purpose	Financial System & management and interface with Government	Performance improvement plan	SWOT Analysis	Problems encountered	Strategic initiatives
										100 per cent metering
										T&D lines in the state are being modernized and augmented
										IPPs' participation hydel power generation about 25 mw through joint ventures to ensure 14 % return and 10-12 % free power

(Contd.)

ANNEXURE 1.7: (Contd.)

Name of SLPE and Year of establishment	*Form of Organisation*	*Market Structure (MS) and Activities (A)*	*Financial Status and Physical performance*	*Employees*	*Social purpose*	*Financial System & management and interface with Government*	*Performance improvement plan*	*SWOT Analysis*	*Problems encountered*	*Strategic initiatives*
State Power Dev. Corp. (1998)	Government Company	MS: Non Competitive A: Exploit state hydro power potential, undertake pre-feasibility studies of Hydro power Projects, Survey and investigating work relating to hydro power projects	Inadequate equity support, high salaries, dues on purchase of power of Rs 8.5 crore	21 Mgl: 7 Ngl: 14	Generating power at economical rates for the consumption of masses	Interface with government: low	VRS for excess employees, Capacity building process	S: promoting hydro power projects through public private partnership, Experienced Manpower	Lack of seed money, non-extensions of govt. guarantees and retention of micro, mini and small hydro power projects	Financial restructuring of Energy and power department
		Other activities; Arranging finances for the power projects through (PFC, IRDA,NABARD, ADC) and Generation of Hydro Power	Pending bills of supplier/ contractor of Rs 9.5 crore					W: Weak equity base		Transfer of assets, liabilities and personnel of energy and power department

(Contd.)

ANNEXURE 1.7: (Contd.)

Name of SLPE and Year of establishment	*Form of Organisation*	*Market Structure (MS) and Activities (A)*	*Financial Status and Physical performance*	*Employees*	*Social purpose*	*Financial System & management and interface with Government*	*Performance improvement plan*	*SWOT Analysis*	*Problems encountered*	*Strategic initiatives*
								O: Becoming a hydro power consultancy and power generation		To make the corporation sustainable GoS may pass on free power from the existing and new hydro power project till it attains break-even
								T: Govt. policy to promote IPPs and indecision on retaining/ divesting power departments of power project		

(Contd.)

ANNEXURE 1.7: (Contd.)

Name of SLPE and Year of establishment	Form of Organisation	Market Structure (MS) and Activities (A)	Financial Status and Physical performance	Employees	Social purpose	Financial System & management and interface with Government	Performance improvement plan	SWOT Analysis	Problems encountered	Strategic initiatives
Sikkim Co-operative Milk Union Ltd (1980)	Co-operative Enterprise	MS: Competitive A: Milk procurement, cattel development, feed and fooder distribution, milk processing and milk market	Loss making company, receding net worth, negative working capital,	83 Mgl. 7 and Nmgl 60, Casual 16	uplift socio-economic conditions of the milk producers	Vision: Diary farmers' prosperity through consumern satisfaction and good and effective MIS system	Perodic review of key performance indicators	S: Abundant live stock wealth, established milk producers co-operative society, established network of milk retail outlet and good networks of retail products	Inadequate advertising expenses	Product portfolio restructuring by adding new products such as Panner, Chrpi, Cream,
			Physical performance: 60 % capacity utilisation		Enhance the milk yeild of the milch animals	Right sizing implemented by giving VRS to 22 employees costing 1.13 crore		W: High transportation and establishment costs; un trained manpower	High establishment cost	Market Restructuring: market milk distribution is been outsourced, milk parlors in Gangtok and other towns, better packaging of milk and milk products

(Contd.)

ANNEXURE 1.7: (Contd.)

Name of SLPE and Year of establishment	Form of Organisation	Market Structure (MS) and Activities (A)	Financial Status and Physical performance	Employees	Social purpose	Financial System & management and interface with Government	Performance improvement plan	SWOT Analysis	Problems encountered	Strategic initiatives
					Provide rural employment	Competitive prices,		O: Capability to produce milk and milk products, boost to export potential due to opening of Nathalie trade route, abundant fooder grass/ tree fooder	High transportation cost	Financial Restructuring: Internal audit systems to be introduced
					Capacity building of farmers	Inadequate costing and internal audit system		T: Local milk vendors, inroads into the local market by mega co-operatives and MNCs	Low per capita milk production	Manpower restructuring: VRS to surplus employees and appointment of qualified manpower, more vigorous capacity building programmes

(Contd.)

ANNEXURE 1.7: (Contd.)

Name of SLPE and Year of establishment	Form of Organisation	Market Structure (MS) and Activities (A)	Financial Status and Physical performance	Employees	Social purpose	Financial System & management and interface with Government	Performance improvement plan	SWOT Analysis	Problems encountered	Strategic initiatives
						Interface with the Government: moderate			One-time collection of milk	Technological Restructuring: effective cold chain maintenance, automation of milk testing procedures, computeri-sation of all at work levels
									Closer of milk societies in monsoons	
									Entry of MNCs and major co-operatives	

Source: Based on Interactions with the Chief Executives of the SCPEs in Sikkim, Policy Makers and Researchers.

ANNEXURE 1.8

SUBSIDIES OF SLPEs

Name of the Enterprise	*2001-02*	*2002-03*	*2003-04*
SIDICO	0	0	0
State Bank of Sikkim	0	0	0
Sikkim State Co-operative Bank	0	0	0
Sikkim Jewels	0.24	0.24	0.24
Sikkim Hatchery	0	0	0
Sikkim Poultry	0	0	0
Sikkim Precision Industries	0	0	0
SITCO	0	0	0
Tea Board of Sikkim	0	0	0
Sikkim Milk Union	0.62	0.25	0.34
Govt. Fruit Preservation Factory	0	0	0
Sikkim Tourism	0	0	0
Sikkim Handloom and Handicrafts Dev. Corp. Ltd.	0	0	0
Khadi and Village Board	0	0	0
State Trading Corp.	0	0	0
Sikkim Consumer Co-operative Society	0	2.98	0
SIMFED	0	0	0
Denjong	0	0	0
Sikkim Nationalised Transport Corp.	0	0	0
State Energy and Department of Power	0	0	0
Sikkim Power Dev. Corp.	0	0	0
SABCCO	0	0.34	0.26
Total	0.86	3.81	0.84

0 – Not available.

Source: Annexure 1.9.

ANNEXURE 1.9

QUESTIONNAIRE

Financial and other related Information on SLPEs

I. GENERAL INFORMATION

01a. Name of the enterprise: ____________________
(Please write in BLOCK LETTERS)
01b. Date of formation: ____________________
01c. Name and Designation of the Chief Executive Officer:_____
____
02. Address: ____________________
Pin Code: __________ Tel:__________
Fax: __________ Telex: __________
E-mail: __________
03. Location of Registered Office:____________________
04a. Major lines of activity (put √ mark against the activitiy)

Manufacturing,	*Trading & Services*	*Financial,*	*Promotional*	*Utility*	*Welfare*
[ ]	[ ]	[ ]	[ ]	[ ]	[ ]

04b. Major reasons for establishment:
04c. Description of the Product
05a. Year of promotion: __________
05b. If there was a time lag, please give reasons:
06. Holding company:_______ Subsidiary company: _______
07. Objectives:
08. Form of organisation (Please "tick"):
– Government company
– Public corporation
– Statutory Board
– Statutory or regulatory authority
– Departmental enterprise
– Cooperative society
– Registered society
09a. Give details of Market structure: Monopoly/Competitive

II. GROWTH AND DEVELOPMENT

1. Periodisation (please describe in terms of specific landmark development)
2. Salient Features

III. SOCIAL PURPOSE

1. Major line of social activities undertaken by the organisation
2. Details on outflow of funds for the social activities

S.N	Details	2001-02	2002-03	2003-04	2004-05	Projected

IV. FINANCIAL INFORMATION

(Rs. in lakhs)

S.No.	Details	2001-02	2002-03	2003-04	2004-05	Projected
1.	Equity					
2.	Long-term debt					
3.	Total Investment					
3.	Reserves					
4.	Surplus/losses (-)					
6.	Current Assets					
7.	Current liabilities					
8.	Working capital					
9.	Capital employed (4+8) (This may be calculated on alternate basis from the liabilities route)					
10.	Net Sales/Turnover					
11.	Accumulated Losses					
12.	Net Worth					
13.	Other income					
14.	Total income					
15.	Direct Costs					
16.	Contribution (10-15)					
17.	Gross Margin					
18.	Cost of Sales					
19.	Operating Profit					
20.	Interest					
21.	Profit Before Tax					

S.No.	Details	2001-02	2002-03	2003-04	2004-05	Projected
22.	Tax					
23.	Net Profit					
24.	Subsidies					
	1. Capital					
	2. Revenue					
	3. Managerial					
	4. Hidden					
	5. Total					
25.	Guarantees					
26.	Contingent Liabilities					
27.	Liabilities to be settled					
28.	Valuation of Enterprise					
	1. Land					
	2. Plant Machinery					
	3. Stocks					
	4. Patents					
	5. Liabilities					
	6. Total					
29.	Court Cases					
30.	Contribution					
	1. Interest					
	2. Dividends					
	3. Excise					
	4. Surpluses					
	5. Exports					
	6. Sales Tax					
	7. Depreciation					
	8. Write-Off					

V. PHYSICAL PERFORMANCE

1. Installed Capacity
2. Capacity Utilised
3. Manpower

   Managerial Non-Managerial Casual
4. New Products/ Services Added
5. No. of employees availing VRS
6. Costs incurred on VRS
7. Costs reimbursed on VRS

VI. ORGANISATIONAL STRUCTURE

1.	Size of Board a) Government nominee(s) b) Nominee(s) of Financial Institutions c) Nominee(s) of Workers / Managers d) Nominee(s) of Foreign Collaborators e) Functional directors f) Professional part-time directors g) CMD h) Total (Sanctioned strength of Directors) i) Tenure of the Board of Directors					
2.	What is your Organisational Chart?					
3.	Extent of Delegation & Decentralisation					
4.	Do you practice Internal Audit					
5.	Do you have Budgeting Process					
6.	What are your Investment Policies					
7.	What Pricing methods are followed?					
8.	Do you have Man Power Planning & Performance Appraisal					
9.	Training Programmes					
10.	Status of R&D					
11.	What Performance Evaluation Methods are followed?					

VII. SWOT Analysis

1. Strengths
2. Weaknesses
3. Opportunities
4. Threats

VIII. RESTRUCTURING

Give details on the following aspects:

1. Product portfolio
2. Market Restructuring
3. Financial Restructuring
4. Manpcwer Restructuring
5. Organisational Restructuring

6. Technological Restructuring
    1. What is the average tenure for the Board of Directors?
    2. What is the existing Compensation Package offered to the CEO and Board of Directors?

IX. STRATEGIC INFORMATION

1. Is your enterprise involved in:
    (i) Restructuring
    (ii) Disinvestment
    (iii) Privatisation
2. Indicate the financial costs of (including VRS, Settlement of Liabilities, rate of sale of assets, etc.)
    (i) Restructuring
    (ii) Disinvestment
    (iii) Privatisation
3. Indicate the social costs of:
    (i) Restructuring
    (ii) Disinvestment
    (iii) Privatisation
4. Provide the proposed steps for:
    (i) Restructuring
    (ii) Disinvestment
    (iii) Privatisation

1. What is the market structure of the organisation?
2. Please provide the Company's Profile?
3. Give Details on Foreign Collaborations.
4. What is the present state of Technology?
5. What is the extent of spending on Advertising Expenses?
6. What is the share in Exports and Imports?
7. Please give Details on any Mergers and Acquisitions taken place?
8. What is your Corporate Vision?

Please provide exhaustive notes on:

1. Valuation of assets.
2. Privatisation, closure and restructuring of activities, divisions, products/services, enterprise.
3. Problems faced by the enterprise.
4. How the enterprise proposes to meet the resource gap in the future due to the reduction in budgetary support by the Government.
5. Details of VRS in existence at present, and details concerning the number of employees accepting VRS, total incidence of VRS in monetary terms, and future plan of action.

ANNEXURE 1.10

SCHEDULE ON INTERNAL ORGANIZATION AND STRUCTURE

SECTION 1: BACK GROUND OF THE ENTERPRISE

Table 1: Back Ground

List of Firms	*Objective*	*Legal form*	*Uni-Plant or Multi-Plant*	*Capacity*		*Major products/ Activities*	*Turnover: product wise or Activity wise*	*Employee Strength*	*Market Structure*	
				Installed	*Utilisation %*	*Managerial*	*Non-Managerial*	*Total*	*% of Mgrl. to Total*	*% of Non-Mgrl. To Total*

SECTION 2: ORGANISATION STRUCTURE

Table 1: Number and Tenure of the Board

List of firms	*Number of Board of Directors*										*Average Tenure of the Board*							
	Initially					2003-04					Initially				2003-04			
	1	2	3	4	T	1	2	3	4	T	1	2	3	4	1	2	3	4

Note: 1 – Government Officials (Bureaucrats), 2 – Politicians, 3 – SLPE Personnel, 4 – Labour representative, and 5 – Total.

Table 2: Changes in CEO and Functional Directors

List of Firms	Number of Changes in Chief Executive Officers(CEOs) & Functional Directors(FDs)									
	CEO	FD	CEO	FD	CEO	FD	CEO	FD	CEO	FD

Table 3: Frequency of Changes

List of Firms	Chief Executive Officer				Functional Director			
	Once in 3 years	Once in 2 years	Once in 1 year	Twice or more in 1 year	Once in 3 years	Once in 2 years	Once in 1 year	Twice or More in One Yr.

Table 4: BOD Meeting and Percentage of Attendance

List of Firms	1992-93				1993-94				1994-95				1995-96				1996-97			
	1	2	3	4	1	2	3	4	1	2	3	4	1	2	3	4	1	2	3	4

Note: 1 – Total Number of Directors, 2 – Total BOD Meetings Held, 3 – Number of Directors Attended, and 4 – Percentage of Attendance – (3÷1) × 100.

Table 5: Decision-Making Powers – Pricing

List of Firms	Govmnt. (✓)			BoD (✓)			CEO (✓)			Others (✓)		
	1	2	3	1	2	3	1	2	3	1	2	3

Note: 1 – At the Time of Inception, 2 – Currently, and 3 – Year When Changed.

Table 6: Decision-Making Powers – Investment

List of Firms	Govmnt. (✓)			BoD (✓)			CEO (✓)			Others (✓)		
	1	2	3	1	2	3	1	2	3	1	2	3

Note: 1 – At the Time of Inception, 2 – Currently, and 3 – Year When Changed.

Table 7: Decision-Making Powers – Hiring of Labour/Officials

List of Firms	Govmnt. (✓)			BoD (✓)			CEO (✓)			Others (✓)		
	1	2	3	1	2	3	1	2	3	1	2	3

Note: 1 – At the Time of Inception, 2 – Currently, and 3 – Year When Changed.

Table 8: Decision-Making Powers – Retrenchment/Suspension of Labour/Officials

List of Firms	Govmnt. (✓)			BoD (✓)			CEO (✓)			Others (✓)		
	1	2	3	1	2	3	1	2	3	1	2	3

Note: 1 – At the Time of Inception, 2 – Currently, and 3 – Year When Changed.

Table 9: Decision-Making Powers – Collaboration with Foreign Firms

List of Firms	Govmnt. (✓)			BoD (✓)			CEO (✓)			Others (✓)		
	1	2	3	1	2	3	1	2	3	1	2	3

Note: 1 – At the Time of Inception, 2 – Currently, and 3 – Year When Changed.

Table 10: Decision-Making Powers – Collaboration with Other Firms within Country

List of Firms	Govmnt. (✓)			BoD (✓)			CEO (✓)			Others (✓)		
	1	2	3	1	2	3	1	2	3	1	2	3

Note: 1 – At the Time of Inception, 2 – Currently, and 3 – Year When Changed.

SECTION 3: GOVERNMENT CONTROL

Table 1: Interaction of CEO/Senior Level Officers with Political Entities

List of Firms	Ministers			Ministers of State			MLAs			Chairperson (If Political)			Others		
	Last I mnth.	Last 6 mnths.	Last 1 yr.	Last I mnth.	Last 6 mnths.	Last 1 yr.	Last I mnth.	Last 6 mnths.	Last 1 yr.	Last I mnth.	Last 6 mnths.	Last 1 yr.	Last I mnth.	Last 6 mnths.	Last 1 yr.

Table 2: Instructions from Political Entities to CEOs/Senior Officers(SOs)

List of Firms	Ministers			Ministers from State			MLAs			Chairperson (If Political)			Others		
	Last I mnth.	Last 6 mnths.	Last 1 yr.	Last I mnth.	Last 6 mnths.	Last 1 yr.	Last I mnth.	Last 6 mnths.	Last 1 yr.	Last I mnth.	Last 6 mnths.	Last 1 yr.	Last I mnth.	Last 6 mnths.	Last 1 yr.

Table 3: Frequency of Receiving Instructions (Past Six Months)

List of Firms	Pricing					Investment					Personnel selection					Purchase of Inputs					Other daily Decisions				
	1	2	3	4	5	1	2	3	4	5	1	2	3	4	5	1	2	3	4	5	1	2	3	4	5

Note: 1 – Ministers, 2 – Ministers of State, 3 -- MLAs, 4 – Chairpersons (Political), and 5 – Others.

Table 4: Interaction of Enterprise with Government Officers

List of Firms	Rank-1			Rank-2			Rank-3			Rank-4		
	Last 1 Mnth.	Last 6 Mnths.	Last 1 year	Last 1 Mnth.	Last 6 Mnths.	Last 1 year	Last 1 Mnth.	Last 6 Mnths.	Last 1 year	Last 1 Mnth.	Last 6 Mnths.	Last 1 year

Table 5: Receipt of Information from Government Officers

List of Firms	Rank-1			Rank-2			Rank-3			Rank-4		
	Last 1 Mnth.	Last 6 Mnths.	Last 1 year	Last 1 Mnth.	Last 6 Mnths.	Last 1 year	Last 1 Mnth.	Last 6 Mnths.	Last 1 year	Last 1 Mnth.	Last 6 Mnths.	Last 1 year

Table 6: Instructions Received from CEO from Government Officers Leading to Decision-Making

List of Firms	Pricing				Investment				Personnel Selection				Purchase of Inputs				Other Daily Decisions			
	R1	R2	R3	R4	R1	R2	R3	R4	R1	R2	R3	R4	R1	R2	R3	R4	R1	R2	R3	R4

Note: R1, R2, R3 and R4 denote the different ranking Government Officers.

SECTION 4: FINANCIAL MANAGEMENT

Table 1: Budgetary Support from Government and Others

(Rs. in lakhs)

List of Firms	Initial			1992-93			1993-94			1994-95			1995-96			1996-97		
	G	O	T	G	O	T	G	O	T	G	O	T	G	O	T	G	O	T

Table 2: Government Equity Extended to Debt Equity

(Rs. in lakhs)

List of Firms	1992-93			1993-94			1994-95			1995-96			1996-97		
	GE	TE	%	GE	TE	%	GE	TE	%	GE	TE	%	GE	TE	%

Source: GE – Government Equity, TE – Total Equity of share holders, and % – (GE/TE) x 100.

Table 3: Long Term Debt as Percentage to Total Debt

List of Firms	1992-93			1993-94			1994-95			1995-96			1996-97		
	LD	TD	%	LD	TD	%	LD	TD	%	LD	TD	%	LD	TD	%

Debt: LD – Long Term Debt, TD – Total Debt, and % – LD/TD x 100.

Table 4: Subsidy

List of Firms	1992-93					1993-94					1994-95					1995-96					1996-97				
	C	R	M	H	T	C	R	M	H	T	C	R	M	H	T	C	R	M	H	T	C	R	M	H	T

Subsidy: C – Capital, R – Revenue, M – Managerial, H – Hidden*, and T – Total.
* includes concessional interest rates charged by Govt., interest free loans extended by Govt., Dividends foregone by the Govt., plant and land given by Govt. etc.

Table 5: Cash Profit/Losses

List of Firms	1992-93	1993-94	1994-95	1995-96	1996-97
	Rs.	Rs.	Rs.	Rs.	Rs.

Table 6: Gross Margin

List of Firms	1992-93				1993-94				1994-95				1995-96				1996-97			
	GM	%GM	%OM	SAT y/n	GM	%GM	%OM	SAT y/n	GM	%GM	%OM	SAT y/n	GM	%GM	%OM	SAT y/n	GM	%GM	%OM	SAT y/n

GM – Gross Margin, % GM – % of Gross Margin, % OM – Optimal % of GM, SAT – Satisfied with the % of GM, Yes or No?

Table 7: Cost Management

List of the Firms	Are your Labour Costs:			Have You Introduced/ Undertaken the Following: Yes(y) or No(n)							
	High/ Low	Comparable to Similar Enterprises in Private Sector (✓)	What is the Ideal % of Spending on Labour?	Cost Sheet	Standardised your Costs	Variance Analysis	Cost Control System	Cost Reduction Programme	ABC	EOQ	VE

ABC – ABC analysis (Inventory Control), EOQ – Economic Order Quantity (Inventory Control), VE – Value Engineering.

Table 8: Budgetary Support from Government, Banks and Financial Institutions

(Rs. in Lakhs)

Firms	1992-93					1993-94					1994-95					1995-96					1996-97				
	GE	B/FI	O	TE	%GE	GE	B/FI	O	TE	%GE	GE	B/FI	O	TE	%GE	GE	B/FI	O	TE	%GE	GE	B/FI	O	TE	%GE
FINANCIAL																									
COMMERCIAL																									
PROMOTIONAL																									

GE – Government Equity, B/FI – Banks/Financial Institutions, O – Others, TE – Total Equity, % GE – % of GE to TE.

Table 9: Hidden Subsidies

(Rs. in Lakh)

Firms	1992-93	1993-94	1994-95	1995-96	1996-97	Total
FINANCIAL						
SUB						
COMMERCIAL						
SUB						
PROMOTIONAL						
SUB						
TOT						

Table 10: Long-Term Loans From Government, Banks/FIs

(Rs. in lakhs)

FIR MS	1992-93				1993-94				1994-95				1995-96				1996-97			
	G	B	T	%	G	B	T	%	G	B	T	%	G	B	T	%	G	B	T	%
FINANCIAL																				

(Contd.)

Table 10: (*Contd.*)

COMMERCIAL																				
PROMOTIONAL																				

SECTION 5: SIGNIFICANT CHANGES

Table 1: Significant Changes

List of Firms	***Restructuring***			*Professionalisation of Board (y or n)*	*Disinvestment/Privatisation/ Others*
	Financial (y or n)	*Labour (y or n)*	*Organisational (y or n)*		

ANNEXURE 1.11

VALUATION OF SLPEs AS ON MARCH 31, 2004

Name of the Enterprise	Land & Building	Plan & Machinery	Stocks	Sundry Debtors	Others	Cash Bank balance and investments	Sundry creditors	Total
SIDICO	0.21		0.82		10.30	7.06		18.39
State Bank of Sikkim	10.02			21.1		185		216.12
Sikkim State Co-operative Bank *	0	0	0	0	0	0	0	0
Sikkim Jewels	0.27	0.5	1.52	0.65			0.27	2.67
Sikkim Hatchery	1	0.75	0.5	0.25				2.5
Sikkim Poultry	0.7							0.7
Sikkim Precision Industries	0.69	2.3	0.17	0.08	4.38			7.62
SITCO	0.71	14.29	4.57	2.59	0.07		0.4	23.15
Tea Board of Sikkim	4.35	0	0	0	0	0	0	4.35
Sikkim Milk Union	0.05	0.8	0.13					0.98
Govt. Fruit Preservation Factory	1	1.5	0.5	0.12				3.12
Sikkim Tourism	3.27	0	0	0.25			2.3	3.52
Sikkim Handloom and Handicrafts Development Corp.	0.93	0.22	0.08					1.23
Khadi and Village Board	0	0	0	0.58	1.45	0	0	2.03
State Trading Corp.	0.03	0	3.81	0	28.66	0	0	32.5
Sikkim Consumer Co-operative Society	0.9	0.2	0.4	0.82	0	0	0	2.32
SIMFED*	0	0	0	0	0	0	0	0
Denjong	0.52	0	0.03	0	0.16	0	0	0.71
Sikkim Nationalised Transport Corp.	84.78	22	3	3.5	6.05		2	117.33
State Energy and Department of Power*	0	0	0	0	0	0	0	0
Sikkim Power Dev. Corp.*	0	0	0	0	0	0	0	0
SABCCO	0	0	0	0	1.43	0	0	1.43
Total	109.22	43.48	14.71	29.94	42.2	192.06	4.97	**426.50**

* Estimates not available.

ANNEXURE 1.12

RESTRUCTURING COST AS ON MARCH 31, 2004

(Rs in Crore)

Name of the Enterprise	Severance/ VR	Training	Renovation/ Expansion	Write off	IT requirement	Court cases	Bank overdraft	Repayment of loans	Contingent liabilities	Operational deficit	Advertisement & Promotional	Sundry creditors	Guarantees	Other	Dues from Govt.	Working Capital Assistance	Business Development	Total
SIDICO	0.90	0.15	20.00	13.84	0.10	0	0	0.37	0	0	0.30	0	0	0	0.09	0	0	35.75
State Bank of Sikkim	5.60	0	0	25.24	0	0	0	0	2.14	0	0	0	4.37	0	0	0	0	37.35
Sikkim State Co-operative Bank	0	0	0	0	0	0	0	0	0	0	0	0	0	0	0	0	0	0.00
Sikkim Jewels	4.37	0.5	10.5	0	0.5	0	0	0	4.45	0	0	0.27	0	0.43	0.24	0	0	21.26
Sikkim Hatchery	0.15	0	3	0	0.5	0	0	0	0.45	0.1	0.1	0	0	0	0.5	0.4	0	5.20
Sikkim Poultry	0.06	0.15	1.5	0	0	0	0	0	0.1	0.1	0	0	0	0	0	0	0	1.91
Sikkim Precision Industries	2.1	0.20	1.39	0.11	0	0	0	0.1	0	0	0.1	0	0	0	0	0	0	4.00
SITCO	2.19	0.35	2.85	1.5	0.3	0	5.77	0.51	0	2.54	1.8	0.4	5	0	0	0	0	23.21
Tea Board of Sikkim	0	0	0.72	0	0	0	0	0	0	0	0	0	0	0	0	0	0	0.72
Sikkim Milk Union	1.13	0	0.11	0	0.17	0	0	0.05	0.30	1.61	0	0	0	0	0	0	0	3.37
Govt. Fruit Preservation Factory	0.63	0	0.99	0	0	0	0	0	0	0	0.15	0	0	0	0	0	0	1.77
Sikkim Tourism	0.33	0.35	2.5	0	1.25	0	0	0	1.05	0.65	0.4	2.3	0	0	0	0	0	8.83
Sikkim Handloom and Handicrafts Development Corp. Ltd	0	0.5	0.07	0	0	0	0	0	0.01	0.05	0	0	0	0	0	0	0	0.63

(Contd.)

ANNEXURE 1.12: (Contd.)

Name of the Enterprise	Severance/ VR	Training	Renovation/ Expansion	Write off	IT requirement	Court cases	Bank overdraft	Repayment of loans	Contingent liabilities	Operational deficit	Advertisement & Promotional	Sundry creditors	Guarantees	Other	Dues from Govt.	Working Capital Assistance	Business Development	Total
Khadi and Village Board	0.65	0.1	0.23	0	0	0	0.34	0	0	0	0.02	0	0	0	0	0	0.25	1.59
State Trading Corp.	5.4	0.03	0	0	0.07	0	0	0	0	0	0.02	0	0	0	0	0	0	5.52
Sikkim Consumer Co-operative Society	0.81	0.02	0	0.03	0.12	0	0	0	0	0	0.05	0	0	0	0.59	0	0	1.62
SIMFED	0.5	0	8.0	1	0.5	0	0	0	0	0	0	0	0	0	0	10	9.65	29.65
Denjong	0.4	0	3	1	0	0	0	0	0	1	0	0	0	0	0	3	0	8.40
Sikkim Nationalised Transport Corp.	8.8	0.15	25.27	0	0.1	0.1	0	0	0.08	4	0.1	2	0	0	0	0	0	40.60
*State Energy and Department of Power	0	0	0	0	0	0	0	0	0	0	0	0	0	0	0	0	0	0.00
Sikkim Power Dev. Corp.	0.5	0	0	0	0	0	0	0	0	0	0	0	0	0	0	0	0	0.50
SABCCO	0.5	0.15	1	1.5	0.1	0	0	0	0	0	0.25	0	0	1.2	0	0	0.4	5.10
Total	35.02	2.65	81.13	44.22	3.71	0.10	6.11	1.03	8.58	10.05	3.29	4.97	9.37	1.63	1.42	13.40	10.30	236.98

* The department has been excluded from the scope of this study.

ANNEXURE 1.13

SAVINGS FROM PRIVATISATION/WINDING UP OF NINE *SLPEs

Sl. No.	*Particulars*	*2003-04*
1.	Total Investment	78.19
2.	Opportunity Cost (@ 10 % on Total Investment)	7.81
3.	Less Net Profit	0.27
4.	Add Subsidies	3.22
5.	Total (2+3+4)	10.76
6.	Less Dividends	0.11
7.	Gross Direct Cost (5-6)	10.65
8.	Add Guarantees	50.00
9.	Total Cost (7+8)	60.65
10.	Restructuring Cost	24.96
11.	Annual Saving (9-10)	35.69

(* Sikkim Jewels Ltd, Sikkim Hatchery Ltd, Sikkim Poultry Dev. Corp. Ltd, Sikkim Precision Industries, Govt. Fruit Preservation Company, Sikkim Time Corporation, Sikkim Trading Corp., Sikkim Consumer Co-operative Society and Sikkim Power Dev. Corp.)

Index